MILLING
A Complete Course

MILLING

A Complete Course

Harold Hall

SPECIAL INTEREST MODEL BOOKS

SPECIAL INTEREST MODEL BOOKS
P.O. Box 327
Poole
Dorset
BH15 2RG
England
www.specialinterestmodelbooks.co.uk

First published by S.I. Model Boooks Ltd. 2004

Reprinted 2005, 2006

ISBN 1-85486-232-4

Printed and bound in Great Britain by Biddles Ltd, King's Lynn, Norfolk

Contents

Preface

The main purpose of this book is to assist the newcomer to the milling machine to become an experienced beginner. This is achieved by providing a range of projects to complete which together will give sufficient time spent using the machine for this to be accomplished.

The book assumes that the reader already has a good grounding in the use of the centre lathe (the main machine in most workshops) and gives a minimum amount of detail for completing the turned components. However, should the reader feel a need for a greater understanding of using the centre lathe, then the sister book to this "Lathework, a Complete Course - Workshop Practice Series No. 34" would make useful reading.

With the three main projects being quite sizeable, and the items produced of considerable use in the workshop, the book is not just intended for the newcomer to the milling machine. The experienced user should also find the book beneficial, no doubt also gaining some useful tips as well as having the projects to complete.

Coming to terms with operating the milling machine is quite different to that of using the centre lathe. In the latter case the range of machining processes is comparatively large, outside diameter turning, boring, screw cutting, parting off, high precision work, etc.. When using the milling machine the actual machining operation varies little. However, the wide variety of component shapes, before and after machining, is what creates the problems which have to be resolved. The projects in this book aim to give the required quantity and variety for the newcomer to be very much at home using the machine.

Whilst just reading the book will provide much useful information this will be a poor substitute to actually making the items described. The reader is therefore encouraged to make at least most of the items detailed.

Harold Hall
March 2004

Chapter 1

Getting Started

Using the milling machine does not include the range of operations that are available when using the centre lathe as the machining process varies little from task to task. What does vary is the shape of the part being machined creating problems with mounting, machining in the required position and measuring to ensure a correct part is the result. For this reason the book attempts to create progressively more sizeable projects rather than each dealing with a particular process.

When I purchased my first machine, a mid size mill-drill, it was in the early days of these appearing on the market. I soon found that the accessories provided were far from adequate.

Milling cutter chuck

The machine was provided with drill chuck, tilting vice and a sizeable face cutter; apparently, even now, this is the kit of parts most often provided. The absence of any "T" nuts, a fundamental fixing device for the milling machine, prevented me from mounting my vice, a peculiar omission, especially as I had also received a small selection of end mills. However, with some temporary fixings the vice was mounted and

making some "T" nuts became the first project. Immediately, I found that the machining was not progressing well, surely the machine was not that inaccurate. It soon became apparent that the milling cutter was being pulled out of the chuck due to the spiral form of the cutter. Only if I tightened the drill chuck excessively, and then only if I took very light cuts, could I make satisfactory progress.

Having paid some £600 for a lot of machine, it seemed out of proportion to pay £100 plus for such a small item as a milling cutter chuck. Today a chuck can be purchased a little more cheaply, but if you want imperial and metric collets, and or up to 16mm/ 5/8in shank diameter, you will still be paying a large amount when compared to the cost of the machine. Unfortunately, the bad news is that it is quite impossible to manage without one.

An alternative is to use cutter holders, these consist of a taper shank bored to take a single size cutter shank, but as a number of these are required their cost would not be that much different to a cutter chuck. They are also theoretically less accurate, being unable to compensate for differing cutter shank sizes which occur due to the

1. The three common forms of cutters , left to right end mill, mini mill and slot drill.

permitted tolerance in their diameter. Their use is best reserved for mounting any odd size cutter, perhaps a 16mm shank when only a 12mm collet chuck is available.

Milling vice

The vice I received was robust and proved to adequately hold parts within its capacity, although it soon became apparent that its accuracy left much to be desired. Being of substantial construction there was scope for re-machining which I did. However, because of its tilting facility, it was an involved task. As will be seen, a vice is not as essential as is often considered and more will be said on the subject through the book.

If you want to minimise expense then the milling cutter chuck described in the sister book WPS 34 will considerably limit the cost whilst still accommodating a wide

range of shank diameters and types. It will also provide valuable turning experience.

Having obtained your cutter chuck, making the remaining essential items can now commence. You will of course need some cutters and a few other small tools that I will now deal with.

Milling cutters

Basic cutters come in two forms, end mills and slot drills. These have a maximum diameter of 14mm for a 12mm shank and 20mm for a 16mm shank. The most common form has a threaded end to the shank and requires a collet chuck system to suit. I would strongly advise you to adopt this form. Plain shank cutters and suitable collets are becoming more available but they still lack the absolute certainty of the cutter not being drawn from the collet, even if only lightly tightened. One exception is

12

2. An end mill can only plunge by a very small amount due to its inability to cut to the centre. This makes it impracticable for cutting enclosed slots.

the 6mm shank cutter that is not intended for re-sharpening and does come with a plain shank.

End mills have four cutting edges whilst slot drills have only two. As their name implies, slot drills are for milling slots; in particular closed end slots and whilst at a push end mills can be used for the process this is far from ideal. Both forms of cutter should therefore be obtained.

The 6mm shank cutters are different and have 3 cutting edges and function adequately as both end mills and slot drills. These are known as "mini mills", "throw away mills" and other such names.

The three forms can be seen in **Photo 1** that illustrates the basic difference. The end mill on the left has four cutting edges, all of equal length but stopping short of the centre of the cutter. This prevents the cutter being plunged (as can be seen in **Photo 2**) by very much so their use for making enclosed slots is impracticable.

On the right is the two cutting edge, slot drill where it can be seen that one edge is much longer than the other and passes centre. This permits the cutter to cut to the centre and can as a result be plunged to permit the cutting of enclosed slots.

In the middle is a mini mill that has three cutting edges, all of which cut to the centre and can be used both as end mills and slot drills.

Recent developments in cutting tools using replaceable tips (that have been widely available for use in turning for many years) are now becoming available as end mills and face cutters for use on the milling machine. There is though a limit to how small they can be made and conventional cutters in the smaller sizes, especially slot drills, are still required.

A face cutter, often supplied as an accessory with the mill when purchased is useful for machining large areas. They are not though essential and I will comment

13

more about them later.

Measuring equipment

Measuring parts being made on the milling machine is far more difficult than similar tasks on the lathe, and larger dimensions are also likely. Therefore, a 150mm vernier is essential, likewise a dial test indicator for accurately placing the part on the table, and relative to the cutter. An engineer's square (two in some cases) is also useful for positioning parts on the table as will be seen through the book.

Remaining essential items

The remaining essential items, clamping accessories, an angle plate and parallels, are quite simple and I propose that these should be the basis of the projects in the early chapters.

Chapter 2

Tee Nuts

As milling machines vary in size so the "T" slots are bound to differ in size, it is impossible therefore to quote dimmensions. You may like to do some research to establish the particular sizes to suit your machine but that is far from essential, a length of nut at least equal to the width across the "T" should be satisfactory. Also, do not make the width and thickness of the arms of the "T" too close a fit in the slot as small fragments of swarf will make it difficult to slide the nut into place.

Wanting to machine some "T" nuts but without any initially available presents a problem. There are various ways round this, but making two nuts by hand (hack saw and file) would be the simplest way out. If you already have some "T" nuts available, I would still ask you to consider if you have

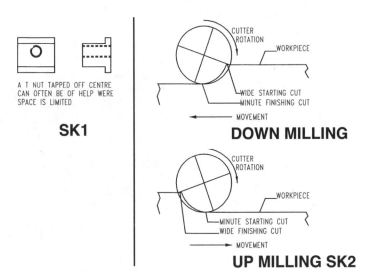

A T NUT TAPPED OFF CENTRE CAN OFTEN BE OF HELP WERE SPACE IS LIMITED

SK1

CUTTER ROTATION
WORKPIECE
WIDE STARTING CUT
MINUTE FINISHING CUT
MOVEMENT

DOWN MILLING

CUTTER ROTATION
WORKPIECE
MINUTE STARTING CUT
WIDE FINISHING CUT
MOVEMENT

UP MILLING SK2

1. Drilling a length of material to make 4 "T" Nuts.

sufficient; 8 would seem the absolute minimum. I would also suggest that some are made with different thread sizes, typically M8 and M10. This may seem a lot but as will be seen, they will find uses beyond what is normally considered to be their purpose. Where space is limited, it is occasionally helpful if the clamping stud could be moved over a little. This can be done by having a few which are tapped off centre, see **SK 1**. If you consider that you have sufficient, please do read this chapter carefully as it deals with the milling operation in more depth than elsewhere in the book.

Making the "T" Nuts

Make two temporary "T" nuts with a thread size one size smaller than that chosen for the nuts to be made, typically, M8 if M10 nuts are envisaged. Cut a length of material for making the number of nuts required including an allowance, say 2mm per nut,

for eventual cutting into individual nuts. The material used should obviously be at least as wide as the chosen width and as deep as the total depth of the nut. It is likely however that the material will have to be over these sizes and the sequence that follows, provides for reducing these dimensions as required. Mark the material out for drilling and tapping, remembering the 2mm allowance, and drill the tapping size holes, **Photo 1**.

Mount the material as shown in **Photo 2** using the two temporary nuts. Whilst this appears to be a simple operation, it immediately becomes apparent that there is more to it than first appears. The clearance of the "T" nut in the slot and the screws in the holes, permits some variation in the position the part takes up. Obviously, the length of material must be true to the axis of the table otherwise the width of the machining will vary end to end. For precision, a dial test indicator in the chuck, or a purpose made mounting, testing along the length of the part as the table is moved is the way to proceed. For this situation

2. Positioning the material on the milling machine table.

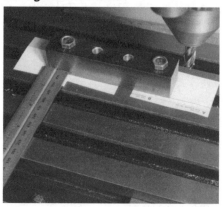

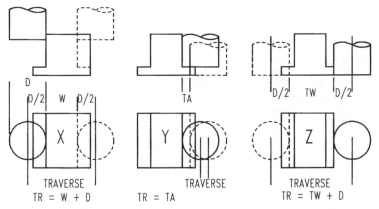

TRAVERSE
TR = W + D

TRAVERSE
TR = TA

TRAVERSE
TR = TW + D

TAKE NOTE OF LEADSCREW BACKLASH WHEN MOVING FROM Y TO Z   **SK3**

though, high accuracy is not that important and a rule dimension at both ends off the front edge of the table will suffice. Note also that the material has been packed up from the table using some thin (0.2mm say) card, the purpose of which becomes apparent later.

Even though you will not be machining more than a few millimetres in width, do use a cutter with a diameter at least three times the width of the cut to be taken; more about the reasoning behind this later.

Up and Down milling

Much written work on the milling process stresses that the movement of the part being machined should oppose the direction of rotation of the cutter. Such terms as Up milling (Climb milling), and Down milling are used and emphasises that the requirement initially stems from horizontal milling. The problem is that when the action of the cutter is attempting to move the part forward in the same direction as it is being fed, a heavy cutting action can suddenly

move the table forward as it takes up the play in the leadscrew. This sudden forward movement will give a dramatic increase in the depth of cut with possible disastrous consequences.

With vertical milling, the light cutting load relative to the table stiffness makes the possibility less likely. Even so, as confidence grows and heavier cuts are taken with larger diameter cutters, it may become a problem, so if no overriding factor exists it is better to conform to the recommendation. However, in industry, where modern machine tables can be backlash free, moving the table with the rotation of the cutter is preferred as it gives a better surface finish. The reason for this is that a cut starts at full depth and reduces to zero whilst in reverse the opposite is the case, **SK 2** attempts to illustrate this.

This is due to the difficulty of making very light cuts unless a cutter has a very fine edge, a situation which would soon be lost with a new cutter even after a small amount of machining. Obviously, after a

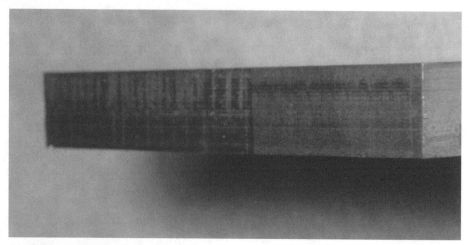

3. Finishes obtained with Up and Down milling compared.

milling cutter has lost its initial fine edge asking the cutter to start cleanly with a minute cut cannot be expected. **SK 2** also attempts to illustrate this.

With the question of up and down milling in mind I decided to carry out a test, making a cut of about 0.1mm depth on a piece of material 10mm thick, doing this in both directions. **Photo 3** shows the result, (on the right), performed using the down milling process; it is much smoother than that on the left using up milling. In the flesh, the part feels almost glass smooth if a finger nail is run along the smoother end whilst it has a rather corrugated feel at the other. You will be given an opportunity to try out this test for yourself later in the series.

Machine speed

Before starting, machine speed must be set. As in turning, the acceptable speed is dependant on many factors: size and sharpness of cutter, type of material, robustness of machine, use, or not, of coolant, etc.. Also, the level of rigidity of the part mounted on the machine table is an important element. This combination of factors precludes the provision of precise rules. With experience it will soon be found that there is more tolerance to the speed chosen than one is often lead to believe.

As a starter I would make the following recommendation; at 12mm diameter, machining mild steel, set the speed at 500 rpm. From here, the important point to remember is that cutter peripheral speed should be the same for all diameters, so at 6mm make the speed 1000 rpm and at 24mm diameter 250 rpm. For aluminium double these speeds and for cast iron and bronze halve them. Of course these speeds will not be exactly available on your machine so select the closest possible. With experience you will no doubt be happy to increase these values, probably quite substantially, although for smaller cutters the top speed of the machine will be the limiting factor.

18

4. Taking the first cut along the length of "T" nut material.

Machining commences

With the machine running, slowly lower the cutter onto the top of the material until first signs of machining appears, move the table to clear the cutter from the part and lower the cutter by around 2mm. Now bring the cutter up to the side of the material, again until first signs of machining are apparent; do this on the visible side of the material. Marking the side with marking blue improves visibility. Move the table length wise to clear the cutter from the end of the part being machined and stop the machine running.

Knowing the initial width of the material and also the width of the "T" nut to be made, calculate the width of the cut to be taken from each side. Set the cut to reduce the width at one pass, providing this is no more than one third the diameter of the cutter

being used. Also check that you will be observing the rule regarding traverse opposing the cutter rotation. Start up and take the first cut. Slowly traverse the workpiece taking the first cut along the whole length as shown in **Photo 4**. Now return to the start, lower the cutter by a further 2mm and repeat the cut. If you feel very much at home with the 2mm depth of cut this could be increased to 3mm for subsequent cuts. This assumes a cutter of at least 12mm diameter.

As guidance to width and depth of cut using an end mill, consider maximum width of cut to be 1/3 cutter diameter and at this width, depth of cut also up to 1/3 cutter diameter. The depth can be increased somewhat if the width of cut is reduced. These figures do though assume a sharp cutter and a fairly robust machine, typically

5. Finish machining the first arm of the "T" to the correct thickness.

the larger mill/drills. For a smaller machine something rather less will be appropriate, reducing depth rather than width, experience will confirm what is possible.

Continue with further cuts until the thickness of the first arm conforms to the size required, **Photo 5**. Now machine the other side using the same process remembering to machine in the opposite direction. A little more care will be needed as you will be machining on the blind side. To set the width traverse the table by a distance of (W)idth of centre portion of nut plus (D)iameter of cutter, see **SK 3**. Take a shallow and short witness cut to check the width of the nut being produced conforms to that required **Photo 6**. Follow this by repeating the process used for machining the first side. A small mirror, perhaps a dental mirror will be useful to inspect the blind side, BUT ONLY WHEN THE CUTTER IS NOT ROTATING.

Next stage is to reduce the width across the arms of the "T" to that required.

Still working on the blind side traverse the table by the projection of the "T" nut arm and lower the cutter until it just touches the card packing and machine along the outer edge of the arm. Now traverse the cross feed by an amount equal to the width across the T, plus the cutter diameter, (again see **SK 3**) and similarly machine the visible side, **Photo 7**. If you are concerned about

6. Taking a witness cut to check that the width conforms to that required.

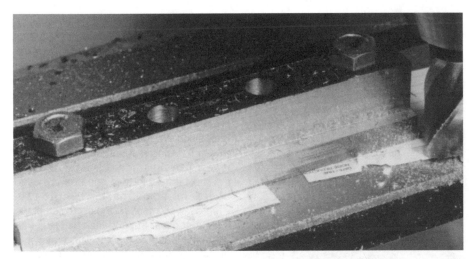

7. Bringing the width across the "T" to size, the card provides a safety margin between the bottom of the cutter and the table face. Below: 8. Reduce the height of the nut over half its length to the required size.

making contact with the machine table see later comment regarding machining the nut end surface. This time you have reversed direction of cross feed so taking account of backlash is a must. An easy way to do this where absolute accuracy is not a requirement, as in this case, is to lock the

cross feed table when setting the previous position. At this stage reverse the feed handle until resistance is felt, (which takes up the backlash), then note the feed dial reading, loosen the table lock and feed by the amount as above.

Now to reduce the height of the nut, re-fix the nuts to the table using two fixings in one half of the material length. This will permit half of the nuts to be reduced in height at the first attempt. Remember, width of cut should not be greater than one third cutter diameter. In practice, and this would be an excellent test to carry out at a later time, it will be found that, at an appreciable depth of cut, traversing requires very much more force on the leadscrew handwheel as the width of cut approaches half cutter diameter, or greater. As I see this, although I have never seen it explained this way, it is because movement of the cutter's cutting edge at one point is at right angles to the

9. An engineers square in an excellent aid to positioning items on the machine table.

direction of traverse of the part being machined (**SK. 4**). In theory this is impossible but can occur if the cutter is momentarily deflected, hence the increased force required at the feed handwheel. After one pass return the cutter to the beginning, place on a further cut and repeat the process. Repeat the procedure to complete the machining, **Photo 8**.

If you are being ambitious and making a large number of nuts, it may be safer to first clamp over two thirds of the length and machine one third at a time. An alternative would be to use side supports but, in theory at least, you have no "T" nuts to hold these. Remove the part from the machine table and refit to enable the other end to be machined in a similar fashion.

Finally cut the length into individual nuts and machine the ends. Of course, the nuts will work perfectly adequately with just sawn ends, but we are in this for the experience. Clamp the first nut to the machine table, again using thin card as packing, and using an engineer's square to position the nut accurately as shown in **Photo 9**. Using a square in this manner is a very useful aid to positioning items on the machine table, two squares are even better in some cases, **Photo 10**. Progressively machine the end by stepping the cutter down the end face as was done along the length of the nut. This time width of cut will only need to be sufficient to remove any saw marks, probably only in the region of 0.5mm. Bearing in mind that this is the first of many ends to be similarly machined, do set the depth stop just short of the table surface! This will avoid the possibility of hitting the machine table in a moments lapse of concentration, easily done when many similar parts are being produced. At this early stage in your experience with a milling machine, you may like to err on the side of caution and set the stop with the cutter a little higher, say 0.1mm. The very thin web left will easily be removed at the deburring stage.

Now the end will still show that machining was done in stages and whilst this is of no real consequence, eliminating these marks will be useful experience. With the cutter still in the lower position set on a further cut, of say 0.1mm, and surface the complete end at one pass. Machining the complete height (probably 15 to 20mm) at one pass may seem that it will present too much side load on the cutter, however, due to the spiral action

10. Two engineers squares can be used to position items in line with table travel.

the actual width of cut will be much less.

For the mathematically minded **SK 5** shows that for a 12mm cutter and a depth of cut of 0.1mm the width of cut will only be 2.3mm. Ideally, a relatively new cutter with its cutting edges still in good condition should be reserved for such applications.

Word of warning

As a word of warning, swarf produced by this process is needle sharp with obvious dangers. Whilst in warning mode, I will also remind readers that milling cutters, especially when new, have razor sharp edges. Because of this they should be held in cloth when screwing them into threaded collets which can be a little stiff if either the threads in the collet, or those on the cutter, are not scrupulously clean.

Ideal practice would be to first finish one end only of each nut. Then, use locating fences (see Photo 3 Chapter 4) to position the nuts for machining the second end. Using this approach will make it easy to ensure all nuts are the same length, not essential but good for experience.

Finishing off

With the machining stages now complete, liberally chamfer all the edges using a file and finally tap them with the required thread. You may chose to leave the nuts in the raw finish or, for a professional finish, oil black them or black them using one of the chemical methods available.

Screws, studs and washers

The "T" nuts must of course be

23

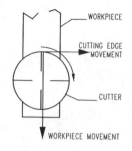

SK4

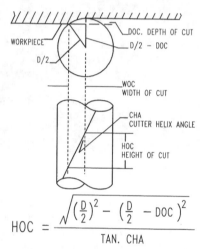

$$HOC = \frac{\sqrt{\left(\frac{D}{2}\right)^2 - \left(\frac{D}{2} - DOC\right)^2}}{TAN.\ CHA}$$

THIS WOULD GIVE FOR –
DEPTH OF CUT DOC = 0.1MM,
CUTTER DIAMETER D = 12MM
CUTTER HELIX ANGLE CHA = 27 DEGREES
A HEIGHT OF CUT HOC OF 2.3MM

SK5

complemented by a supply of studs, screws, nuts and washers. Screws are easier to use than studs with loose nuts, you will though need screws in length increments of 5mm and this is obviously impracticable, therefore studs will be required and could be used exclusively

instead of screws if it was considered an easier option.

Screws, if used say for shorter sizes for holding such items as a vice or an angle plate, should be high tensile. Studding is not likely to be high tensile but providing you have chosen either M8 or M10 this should not be a problem. This is easily available in 300mm or 1M lengths, either from mail order outlets or your local DIY superstore; it can then be cut down to lengths required.

When using studs that have a continuous thread they can pass through the "T" nut and hit the bottom of the "T" slot. When tightening the assembly it is possible for the stud to turn attempting to jack up the side webs of the "T" slot. Some commentators have stated that this can cause the webs to fracture. Personally, looking at the robust nature of the "T" slots on modern machines I find this improbable. As a precaution though the following practice should be adopted. Run the stud into the "T" nut until it bottoms in the "T" slot, then wind it back a couple of turns making sure it does not once more bottom in the slot as the nut is run on. The use of studs being threaded from either end with one just sufficient to enter the "T" nut overcomes the possible problem. These can be purchased at a price but with the wide range of lengths required, making one's own would be a worthwhile exercise.

The use of screws however needs much more caution as whilst the above can still arise, there is also another potential and more serious problem. If the screw is much too long it will be obvious as the item will remain loose on the table when it bottoms in the "T" slot. It is though possible that on the border line it will clamp the part sufficient to appear adequate but will move when the cutting forces are applied. This could have disastrous consequences and apparently in some machine shops the use of screws is taboo. Used with care though, there is no reason for this if the following is adopted as standard practice. Place the screw into the "T" slot and move it close to the item being clamped observing that the head is lower than the item. In this case adequate clamping can be guaranteed but do also ensure that the screw is not so short, that only a thread or two will engage with the nut.

As angle plates, clamps and other items will frequently have slots, large diameter heavy duty washers are a must, as these are not that easy to come by making a small quantity would be a useful exercise on the lathe. Nuts should be high tensile.

Having considered "T" nuts and their associated parts there remain three items: clamp bars, an angle plate, and pairs of parallels in a range of heights. We start with the angle plate in the next chapter.

Chapter 3

An Angle Plate

Machining an angle plate

Introducing the manufacture of an angle plate at this early stage may appear premature. It is though an essential item for much of the work that follows and this dictates that it is covered now. When the subject has been fully studied, and hopefully made, I think you will agree that it is not as daunting a task as may first be thought.

Machining cast iron

Machining cast iron falls into two stages. The outer skin can be extremely hard and without proper precautions can easily destroy the tool being used. However, with the outer skin removed machining is as easy or even easier than mild steel. It does though machine quite differently and it is a very dirty operation. Do therefore use a good barrier cream on your hands.

Choice of tool type is especially important; do not use a precious high speed steel tool as one hard spot and the tool will need sharpening, so this is really a non-starter. Start machining using an elderly cutter that you will not be too concerned about damaging.

Alternatively, an end mill having replaceable tips, as mentioned in Chapter 1, would be an excellent choice (if available) but do ensure the tips are of a suitable grade for the purpose.

Having mentioned the casting's hard surface that can destroy cutters, of any type, care has to be taken to make sure that the method used to machine the component attempts to overcome the problem. It is not an inevitable problem as many castings will machine with ease. The method is to make the first cut sufficiently deep to get below the outer skin where the possible problem lies. However, with castings being of irregular shape, a cut that

1. The angle plate casting with the cylindrical squares and clamp bar necessary to complete its machining.

starts sufficiently deep may subsequently just scrape the surface as the machining progresses; a sure recipe for a damaged tool. Under these circumstances the process should be halted and the tool returned to the start and a deeper cut set.

Having totally removed the surface skin the remaining machining can proceed with ease using a newer cutter with very little more caution than with other materials. Incidentally, it is normal to machine cast iron dry.

Cylindrical square

Machining a precision angle plate from a raw casting without access to a second plate may seem like asking the impossible. The method makes use of two precision squares, a posh name for a round piece of metal having its diameter accurately parallel along its length. The diameter of the squares is not critical, neither do they have to be the same, but to ensure they sit accurately on the machine table a diameter of no less than three times the "T" slot width should be aimed at.

Cylindrical squares should be turned parallel, certainly within 0.005mm, preferably better, and their bases faced immediately after machining their outer diameter without removing them from the lathe. This results in a pillar where the side

2. Removing any hard spots around the edge by machining the edges first.

is precisely square to the base. This is covered in much greater detail in the WPS 34 in the Workshop Practice Series.

The two squares, already mounted, with the angle plate casting (Ref. 1) and an essential clamp bar (only the centre hole is required) are shown in **Photo 1**.

First dress the main faces of the casting with a file to remove any minor projections and test each one on a surface plate. My casting sat on the plate without the slightest rock and this was chosen to mount against squares on the machine table. If this is not the case some additional filing may be necessary or possibly some packing between the casting and the

squares. A thin piece of card could also be used to protect the squares and compensate for any very minor errors in flatness.

Face one

With the casting mounted as in **Photo 2** machining can commence. First completely machine round the casting as shown and by going round anticlockwise the cutter will be breaking out at the casting edge rather than cutting into it. This will have the effect of chipping away at the outer face causing it to break away rather than be cut and having much less drastic effect on the cutters cutting edges. Follow this by taking

3 and 4. (Above and Facing Page) Rough machining the first face.

lengthwise cuts to completely machine the first face as in **Photo 3** and **Photo 4**. Set the tool just a little deeper, say 0.05mm, so as to skim the face created by the initial machining.

Should the cut, due to the irregular surface of a casting, become too shallow to remove the surface skin cleanly, stop the process and repeat the cut made a little deeper as in **Photo 2**. Then a further attempt can be made to machine the first face completely as in Photos 3 and 4. This repeat operation approach may be required with any of the machining operations that follow.

Rough and finish machining
I would point out that, after rough machining the casting fully on all the required surfaces, it will be necessary to essentially repeat the same operations as a finishing stage. All the photographs were taken at the roughing stage but are equally applicable when finishing the casting.

Face two
Remove the casting and reposition again as in Photo 2, with the now machined face against the squares there should be no problem regarding flatness, a check first on the surface plate will be worthwhile though.

Repeat the process used on face one to machine face two. Incidentally, if you make the squares taller than the casting it will be necessary to pack up the casting from the table, this can be seen in Photos 3 and 4. Any suitable piece of metal will suffice, the precision of a genuine parallel in not required.

Ends

Now with the two main faces machined, mount the casting between the two squares, **Photo 5**, and machine the end as shown. To ensure the ends are perfectly square with the two faces it is essential that the faces butt accurately with the squares. Lifting the casting off the machine table will ensure that this third face in no way influences the attempt to achieve this. With the first end completed, turn the casting and mount again in the same way and machine the second end. You may ask why take so much care with the ends, why do they need to be square? It can be seen though in Chapter 7, **Photos 9 & 10**, that it is not unusual to mount an angle plate onto the machine table, end on.

Some question the use of toolmaker's clamps for work holding on machines, but providing they are robust enough, and set

31

5. The cylindrical squares are also used when machining the ends.

correctly, there is no reason why they should not be used. The subject of clamps is discussed in detail in Chapter 6. If you do not posses toolmaker's clamps then with care substantial "G" clamps can be used, otherwise, the clamp bar used in the original set up, together with a second bar could be employed.

The long edges

Finally, at the roughing stage, the two long edges can be machined by the method shown in **Photo 6**.

Finish machining

All materials contain within them stresses that have been introduced at the manufacturing stage. When sections of the material are removed, this destabilises the internal stresses and causes the material to distort. This situation is particularly prevalent with castings, though the effect is not always immediate. It is therefore, preferable to leave the rough machined casting for at least a few days before final finishing.

When considered ready, re-machine all

6. Machining a long edge. 7 (Right) After rough machining the required faces the setups are repeated for final finishing.

machined faces using the same sequence and setups already used. Problems with hard spots at this stage are much less likely and finishing cuts of say 0.2mm deep will be sufficient to give a good surface finish. Do though use a sharp cutter, cast iron at this stage machines very easily. You could speed up the process by working clockwise. gradually working to the middle but I prefer working in straight lines as this gives what I consider to be a better appearance, see **Photo 7**. For appearance sake each pass should be at the same spacing but there is

no need to be precise. Just a single turn of the leadscrew, or 1-1/2 or 2 whatever suits the situation.

End mills versus face cutters

You may ask why have we machined this angle plate using end mills when I commented in Chapter 1 that most Mill/Drills are supplied with a tungsten carbide, face cutter. Theoretically, the face cutter would be ideal for roughing cuts but I was concerned that the rather heavier, cutting action would be too demanding for the

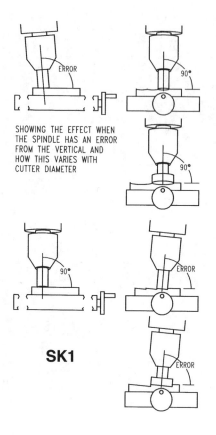

SHOWING THE EFFECT WHEN
THE SPINDLE HAS AN ERROR
FROM THE VERTICAL AND
HOW THIS VARIES WITH
CUTTER DIAMETER

SK1

Rather than attempt to go into detail in the text I have produced **SK 1** that attempts to illustrate the effect of a cutter spindle that is not at 90 degrees to the machine table. The sketch shows that the surface deviations from the flat, depend on whether the error is left to right of back to front. More important though, the larger the cutter used. the greater the effect. In theory therefore the smaller the cutter the flatter the part, in practice though a compromise choice has to be made. Attempting the task using a 4mm end mill would be ludicrous whilst a 50mm face mill would give the greatest error. An end mill 12mm diameter and taking light cuts of about 4mm wide, would be a good compromise.

Finishing touches

Using a file lightly chamfer all edges produced by the machining operations and clean up the slots and their edges. As far as is practical, clean up the remaining unmachined faces of the casting and giving these a lick of paint will give the angle plate a professional appearance.

In the next chapter the subject is Clamps followed by Parallels in the following chapter, after which we get down to some substantial projects.

References

The casting used in the illustrations is Reference No. 501 from The College Engineering Supply, 2 Sandy Lane, Codsall, Wolverhampton, WV8 1EJ Tel/fax 01902 842284.
Website: www.collegeengineering.co.uk. Many suppliers to the modelling and education establishments have similar castings available which would be equally appropriate.

squares mounted on the machine table. This would be the case particularly if they were on the small size in respect to diameter, as were mine.

At the finishing stage the reasons are more obscure. It is easy to assume that the milling machine is perfectly precise in all aspects; they are made to limits though and deviations from the perfect are the norm. Even in toolroom-quality machines, deviations exist, although of course they will be less.

Chapter 4

Clamps

This chapter concentrates on an essential item for use on the milling machine; clamp bars. It would be tempting in the case of the clamps to cut a few short lengths of steel, drill a hole for the clamp stud, deburr, and call it a day. We are in this though for the experience so will aim at a more professional and useful result.

The dimensions on the drawing are for guidance only as size of machine, may dictate the size made. Do though ensure they are sufficiently robust. If in doubt be cautious and use a thicker material, 8mm would seem the minimum for use on the milling machine. The slot and hole will of course have to suit the clamping stud size.

First decide how many are to be made and cut off this number from the bar of material adding 1 - 2mm for final machining.

1. Machining the first end of the clamp, do machine towards the cylindrical square for added security.

As to quantity I would suggest 6 as a minimum. This may seem more than is likely to be used at any one time but as we shall see through the book other uses than direct clamping do frequently occur.

Manufacture

Mount the angle plate and one of the cylindrical squares and first clamp as in **Photo 1**. You will need to make a simple clamp with a single hole if you do not have one. Use one of the other pieces of clamp material as packing for the clamp though it is best practice for the packing to be just higher than the part being held. I normally achieve this by placing a thin piece of card under the part being used as packing but appear not to have done so in this instance.

Machine the top face of the part and, unless you have a large diameter cutter, two passes will be necessary. In all milling operations it is highly desirable to machine towards the supporting items, in this case the cylindrical square. If machining was away from the square, that is from right to left in the photograph, the single clamp may not adequately hold the part. Eagle eyed

2. The positioning screw below the clamp piece enables all the clamps to be easily machined to the same length when machining the second end.

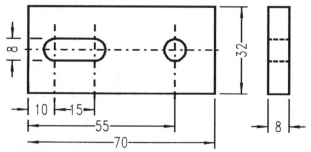

SUGGESTED SIZE ONLY, DIMENSIONS MAY CHANGE TO SUIT MACHINE AND CLAMP STUD SIZES.

SUGGESTED CLAMP DIMENSIONS

3. With the clamp having been marked with the position of the slot, setting the table stops for machining the slot in the first and remaining clamps is easy.

readers may observe that the clamp stud could be higher in the angle plate slot. This would ensure that the clamp held the part nearer the edge being machined for improved security. This is not the case though, as I find that using a "T" nut in the slot enables nuts to be tightened without the need for a second spanner, and often a third hand. The "T" nut does though prevent the screw from being close to the slot end, and I intend to make some with the tapped hole nearer the end which would also be radiused, as in **SK1**, for use in this way; you may like to do the same.

T Nuts, other uses

Having trimmed the first end of all the clamps, machine the second in a similar manner, **Photo 2**. At first this may appear identical to **Photo 1** but closer examination shows that the part is being supported by a screw screwed into a "T" nut, illustrating a point made earlier that there are uses for "T" nuts other than pure clamping. When fitting, turn the screw until it contacts the bottom of the "T" slot and very lightly tighten. This then supports each part as they are fitted onto the angle plate so that each new part can easily be machined to the same length, without recourse to measurement or reading leadscrew dials. A real time saving benefit when a number of identical parts are being made.

Secure clamping

Next mark out the parts for drilling the holes and just one with the extremities of the slot to be made; width and length. Drill the single hole in each one and use this for securing to the machine table as in **Photo 3**. I cannot stress too much, to err very much on the safe side when it comes to securing parts for machining; one too many a clamp is very much better than one to few. With that in mind, placing support pieces which do not actually grip the part will give added security, often in places when an additional direct clamp cannot be applied, typically cases Chapter 6, Photo 9 and Chapter 7, Photo 4.

In this case a single screw fixing would probably suffice, especially as it is a slot being produced that will not tend to place any side load on the item. The support pieces in the photo do though perform a very important additional function. Mount the clamp that had the slot positions marked onto it and position it using an engineer's square off the front face of the machine table. Clamp it in place using the single screw then add the two support pieces as shown in the photograph. As you become more involved in milling machine activities such additional aids to completing the task will become necessary, so do make a habit of keeping these bits and pieces handy for possible future use. Of course the clamps now being made could perform this task for future operations, hence my comment regarding making sufficient.

Fit a slot drill of a size that will cut the slot at one pass. If however a sufficiently wide slot drill is not available, then widen the slot using an end mill as slot drills are too fragile for cutting on one side only. With the machine stationary, lower the cutter so it is almost touching the workpiece. Then, with the cutting edges in line with the cross travel use the cross feed to align the cutter with the marks on the workpiece. Lock the

WHEN USING A T NUT WITH THE FACE PLATE OR ANGLE PLATE, NUTS MADE AS PER THE ABOVE FORM WILL ENABLE BETTER USE OF THE SLOTS TO BE MADE

SK1

cross feed in this position. Now rotate the cutter ninety degrees and traverse the table until the cutting edge lines up with the end mark and set the first table stop (Photo 3) at this point. Knowing the length of the slot set the second table stop with the gap required, and traverse the table to check against the other end mark on the clamp.

Start the machine and plunge the cutter into the workpiece, say by 1mm, and make the first cut. Slot drills can be used in either direction, so plunge the cutter by a further 1mm and take a cut in the reverse direction. Continue until the slot breaks through on the other side. As the slot aligns with the "T" slot there is no danger of the cutter damaging the table surface. The positioning pieces on the table, and the end stops having been set, will make machining the remaining clamps very straight forward.

You may consider that the single hole in the clamp is purely for this machining operation but we shall see later in the book that it has a very important role to play. Generously deburr all edges and the clamps are complete.

Chapter 5

Parallels

A set of parallels are almost as essential as the clamps in the previous chapter for use during milling operations. These could be commercially made items; ones made by the user, or, as so often is the case, just off-cuts from mild steel bar. Whilst in many cases the latter may be adequate, especially when used as a single parallel, two pieces of bar, especially if taken from different lengths of stock material, may not have identical widths. On the other hand the hardened and ground commercial variety will be of accuracy rarely required and be a little on the expensive side. Of more significance though with these, is that they will not be available in a sufficiently wide range of heights if the cost is a consideration. Making your own is a worthwhile option as the cost will be minimal and a wide range of sizes will present no problem. It is possible to buy sets of parallels in 1/8in increments from

1/2 to 1-5/8in and at a very reasonable price. However, many of those available are only 1/8in wide, which is on the thin side especially as some vices have a small grove in their bed adjacent to the fixed jaw. You will also have to trawl the catalogues to find them. Making them still seems a good idea.

Parallel, how?

The aim will be to create parallels in pairs that are both parallel along their length and of exactly the same height, at least within good home workshop standards, say within 0.002mm. At first sight this may appear a standard that is too close to be achieved, especially with regard to being parallel. How, after machining the first side, is the parallel positioned accurately enough for the second to be machined parallel to the first? This is the secret behind the method proposed.

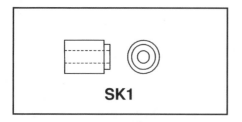

SK1

The heights of the parallels are not critical providing each pair are accurately the same; I would suggest nominal values of 10mm, 15mm, 20mm, 30mm, 40mm and 50mm and say 8mm thick and 100mm long. Having cut your lengths of material, in various widths, machine the ends using the same set-up as in Chapter 4 Photo 1 and generously deburr the ends. Also remove any blemishes along the long faces and edges that could affect the mounting of the pieces for machining.

Make two posts as **SK1**, (as you will see the dimensions are not that critical) and mount these onto the angle plate at approximately the same height. See **Photo 1**. Very lightly machine over the top surface of the posts to give two locating faces for the parallels to sit on. The small, reduced end to the post avoids having to machine too close to the angle plate face. It will be necessary to mount the posts towards the top of the angle plate for the smaller sizes, say 10,15 and 20mm and lower and re-machine them for the larger ones.

The screw seen in the centre slot acts as packing for the clamp when holding the parallels. See **Photo 2**. This should be set at a height just greater than the thickness of the two parallels, say plus 0.5mm. This would seem to be a good time to discuss good practice in terms of clamping and rather than going into great detail in the text, **SK2** should largely cover the subject. However, in this case, if the clamp is not positioned suitably the parallels may tilt with obvious effects on

1. Posts fitted to the angle plate and lightly machined on top enable parallels to be positioned and machined to a fair degree of accuracy.

2. Machining the first side

the height of these, as illustrated in **SK3**. With the first pair of parallels mounted, machine the first side, remove and very lightly deburr edges and ends. Turn over and once more fit in place making sure that the mounting surfaces are scrupulously clean. Machine the second side, **Photo 3**, the piece of packing seen below the clamp

3. Machining the second side

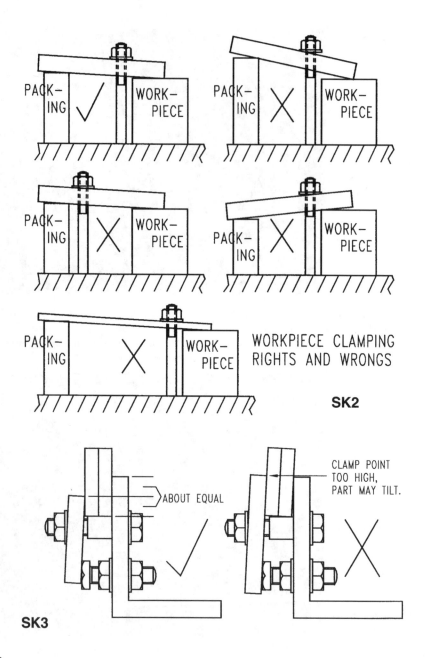

WORKPIECE CLAMPING
RIGHTS AND WRONGS

SK2

ABOUT EQUAL

CLAMP POINT
TOO HIGH,
PART MAY TILT.

SK3

4. Using "T" nuts with an angle plate avoid the need for using a second spanner.

holds this at just the right height. Finally, remove, deburr, and the first pair of parallels are finished. **Photo 4** shows the use of "T" nuts with the angle plate as mentioned in Chapter 4. This avoids the need to use two spanners and frees a hand to help elsewhere.

Without hardening, these parallels will be susceptible to damage to their edges, though if treated appropriately this should easily be avoided. A small wooden tray with separators would help at the storage stage. In any case, damage is likely to be local and can easily be removed with a file without affecting their overall accuracy.

This now completes the basic kit

5. With the basic kit now complete we are ready for some advanced projects.

43

shown in **Photo 5** and through the rest of the book this will be seen to be adequate for completing some sizeable projects without further equipment.

In the next chapter we make a boring head, the first of three substantial projects that bring the book to a conclusion. Even though the projects are quite sizeable the individual machining operations are mostly no more complex than those already met. These projects should not present any major problem, even for the novice, but provide sufficient milling involvement for the newcomer to be well at home with the machine, by the time the three items have been completed.

Chapter 6

Boring Head

The book now moves into projects that will be very useful and at the same time, because of their size, bring considerable satisfaction to the novice on their completion. In the same way that the simple items thus far produced are essential for the manufacture of these major items, so the item in this chapter will be essential for the construction of the second. Likewise, the second is essential for the third item. They are a Boring head, a Dividing Head and a very versatile Grinding Rest.

Material

To simplify material procurement the three items have been designed where possible to use the same material sizes for their major components. Secondly, to ease the machining processes, material sizes that can be obtained free cutting (230M07) have largely been chosen. This limits rectangular shapes to squares only.

Production planning

You may like to expand the purpose of this book into production planning by making this and the remaining items simultaneously. This will enable a particular set-up to be used whilst available for parts in more than one project, reducing the overall time taken quite appreciably. I will of course describe each item as if it is being made in isolation. By now the process of material removal by the milling method should be reasonably well understood and I will therefore keep explanations brief. These final chapters are backed up by a generous number of photographs to illustrate the actual machine set-ups.

The Boring Head
Body (7) and Cutter Carrier (8)
Cut two lengths of 50mm square, 75mm long, plus an allowance for machining. Mount an angle plate and cylindrical

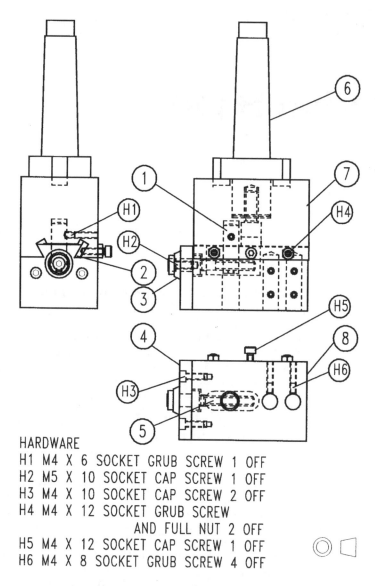

HARDWARE
H1 M4 X 6 SOCKET GRUB SCREW 1 OFF
H2 M5 X 10 SOCKET CAP SCREW 1 OFF
H3 M4 X 10 SOCKET CAP SCREW 2 OFF
H4 M4 X 12 SOCKET GRUB SCREW
              AND FULL NUT 2 OFF
H5 M4 X 12 SOCKET CAP SCREW 1 OFF
H6 M4 X 8 SOCKET GRUB SCREW 4 OFF

BORING HEAD ASSEMBLY

1. Machining the end of the main body. Note the use of the cylindrical square to position the part. Below: 2 Marking out the parts for drilling and slotting.

square, clamp the part ensuring it is accurately in contact with both angle plate and square. Machine the end, **Photo 1**, reverse, then machine the second end to 75mm. Repeat for the second part. This set-

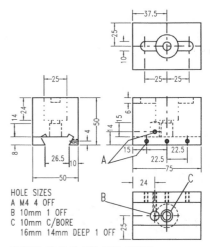

HOLE SIZES
A M4 4 OFF
B 10mm 1 OFF
C 10mm C/BORE
  16mm 14mm DEEP 1 OFF

MATERIAL 50 X 50 MILD STEEL 230M07

QUANTITY 1 OFF

NOTE THE 25mm DIAMETER HOLE WITH 10 mm WIDE SLOTS IS FOR FITTING ARBOR, PART 6, THESE DIMENSIONS MAY REQUIRE CHANGING IF AN EXISTING ARBOR IS TO BE USED.

BODY 7

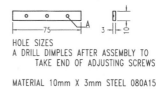

HOLE SIZES
A DRILL DIMPLES AFTER ASSEMBLY TO
  TAKE END OF ADJUSTING SCREWS

MATERIAL 10mm X 3mm STEEL 080A15

QUANTITY 1 OFF

GIB STRIP 2

up ensures that the end faces are truly at right angles to the side faces and parallel to each other; a requirement for a satisfactory conclusion to later operations. Mark out the positions of the holes and the extremities of the slot in the Cutter Carrier, **Photo 2**. Actually, my photograph shows that I did this after reducing the thickness of the carrier to 30mm as detailed later.

49

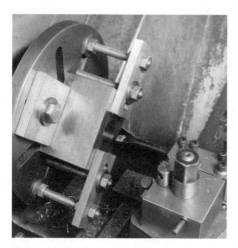

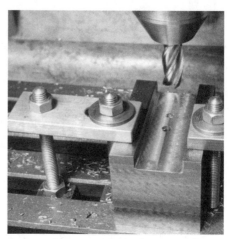

Either method is acceptable but do take note of the eventual reduction in thickness if marking out the carrier at this stage.

Body (7)

Drill pilot holes for B and C. Mount on the lathe faceplate, bore to take the arbor, **Photo 3**. A tailstock centre located in the pilot hole C will accurately position the part on the faceplate whilst clamping. Return the part to the milling machine and mount dovetail side up. Use an engineer's square off the table front edge to accurately position the part. Remove the centre portion to a depth of 8.2mm, working to the dimensions of 10mm and 26.5mm. See **Photo 4.**

In Photo 4 we now see the purpose of the hole in the clamp, that is to take a stud to act as packing. The stud is threaded into a "T" nut (another use for a "T" nut as intimated earlier) and locked with a nut as seen. A nut on the stud below the clamp, not seen, sets the packing height to just higher than the part being held and a further nut placed on top make the assembly secure. This is an excellent packing

Left: 3. Boring the body for the arbor. Right: 4. Preliminary machining of the body prior to machining the dovetails.

method. Note also the use of a substantial washer over the slot.

Loosen the part from its clamps and rotate through 90 degrees, this time allowing the clamps to fall into the recess just made. Skim the slide faces to achieve the 8mm dimension.

Turn over to machine the two 10mm x 6mm slots. Lower the cutter into the 25mm hole and whilst on the 37.5mm centre line, advance the cross slide until the cutter just contacts the bored hole. Lock the cross slide and reverse the handwheel until resistance is felt to take up backlash. Release the cross slide and feed by 7.5mm ((25 − 10)/2). Take a very shallow cut and check to make sure no error has been made, make the two slots at 2mm depth increments. Being an open-ended slot an end mill can be used rather than a slot drill.

At this point it is assumed that as a novice a dovetail cutter is not yet part of

5. An alternative approach to using a dovetail cutter.

the workshop kit, so another method of creating the dovetail is proposed. Even if one were to hand, using the method described would be excellent milling experience.

Mount the angle plate onto the table face end ways on, long clamping studs will be required. (See later Photo 10 for a better view). Again use an engineer's square as accuracy is vital, (using a dial test indicator would be even better). Take a length of steel say 12mm square, though not critical, and about 75mm long, drill in the centre with a hole to take a clamping stud. Fix this onto the angle plate at an angle of 30 degrees, using a stud long enough to also clamp the part.

Fit a 6mm end mill and set this to take an initial depth of cut of 2mm maximum. Remember, at this small size of cutter a high spindle speed will be required, say 1000 rpm plus. Take a first cut adjusting

the cross feed such that a flat of around 0.5mm remains along the length. If previous machining, and the setting of the angle plate at this time is accurate, the flat should be a constant width. If, an appreciable error exists it will be necessary to investigate the reason. A small error, say 0.1mm, is probably inevitable and of no great consequence.

Lower the cutter 2mm at a time until the full depth has been achieved. Follow this by making adjustments to the cross feed of 0.1mm, each time taking a skim along the length; repeat until the flat just disappears. This is a case where direction of traverse can correspond to cutter rotation to achieve the best surface finish, (see Chapter 2, Photo 3)

Remove the part from the angle plate, turn end on end, and repeat the process, **Photo 5**. Remove and place two pieces of rod (about 10mm diameter) one on either side of the dovetail and measure the distance between them at each end. Even if an appreciable error is apparent it is of no consequence, as the Gib Strip will compensate for this. It will though be nice to know the results of your efforts and if the error is less than 0.1mm you have done very well.

Finally, at this stage, drill and tap holes A and finally drill holes B and C.

Leadscrew bearing plate (4)
Cut a piece of steel allowing for subsequent machining, machine the ends, mark out and drill holes A and B. IT IS IMPORTANT to make B, tapping size for M5 at this stage.

Cutter Carrier (8)
Having previously machined the ends, cut the 50mm square to 50mm x 30mm plus to allow for machining to the 30mm dimension. Mount the material onto the

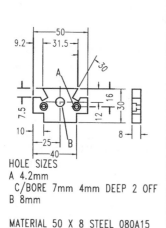

HOLE SIZES
A 4.2mm
 C/BORE 7mm 4mm DEEP 2 OFF
B 8mm

MATERIAL 50 X 8 STEEL 080A15

QUANTITY 1 OFF

LEADSCREW BEARING PLATE 4

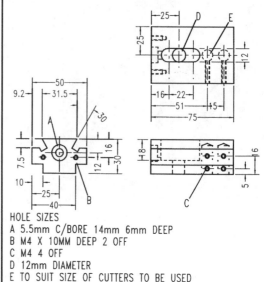

HOLE SIZES
A 5.5mm C/BORE 14mm 6mm DEEP
B M4 X 10MM DEEP 2 OFF
C M4 4 OFF
D 12mm DIAMETER
E TO SUIT SIZE OF CUTTERS TO BE USED

MATERIAL 50 X 50 MILD STEEL 230M07 (50 X 30 IS
              NOT AVAILABLE IN FREE CUTTING 230M07)

CUTTER CARRIER 8

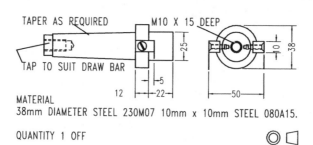

TAPER AS REQUIRED   M10 X 15 DEEP

TAP TO SUIT DRAW BAR

MATERIAL
38mm DIAMETER STEEL 230M07 10mm x 10mm STEEL 080A15.

QUANTITY 1 OFF

NOTE MAY NOT BE REQUIRED IF YOU HAVE AN EXISTING ARBOR.

ARBOR 6

6 and 7. Thicknessing the Cutter Carrier having made it from 50mm sq. Note the cylindrical square is not part of the setup, only left in place for a future task. Below: 8. Positioning the Cutter Carrier for machining the dovetails.

angle plate as in **Photo 6**, sawn side up. Again it is necessary for the angle plate to be aligned with the cross feed. With the ends accurately machined, the part should automatically be parallel with the table's surface lengthwise but needs also to be parallel back to front. Because of this, the use of parallels is essential. It is unlikely that the parallels will be firmly held after clamping the part but do check that the part sits accurately on them and then remove. Machine to 30mm dimension, **Photo 7**.

Drill and tap all holes where required except A; fit the Bearing Plate. Mount the part on the machine table, accurately positioning it aided by a dial test indicator. Machine the 10mm slot guided by the markings previously made, **Photo 8**. Mounting the dial test indicator on some point of the machine, rather than using the drill or cutter chuck, has advantages as it avoids removing a drill or cutter from the chuck that may still need to be used.

Machine the edges as shown in **Photo**

9. Preliminary machining the Cutter Carrier prior to machining the dovetails.

9, in preparation for machining the dovetail, work to the 9.2mm, 31.5mm and 7.5mm dimensions. By way of explanation of the photograph, the clamps were actually made from 1-1/4in material and were therefore just over the 31.5mm width. The pieces of steel either side of the workpiece permit the clamps to be loosened and moved to permit the second side to be machined, without fear of losing accurate positioning of the part. Note also that this necessitated the clamps to rotate a little making it impracticable to locate the packing stud in a "T" nut, as in Photo 4. Using a screw nutted into the clamp and with its head on a piece of packing to overcome the problem, in fact, where the height of the packing is short this is probably as good a method.

Reinstate the angle plate on its end, together with the support bar at 30 degrees, machine following essentially the same process as for the body, see **Photo 10**.

10. Making the dovetails on the Cutter Carrier.

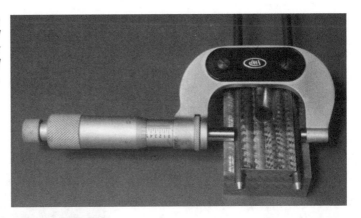

11. Using a micrometer and two rods to check if the dovetail sides are parallel.

12. With the unit partially assembled, the Leadscrew Nut is drilled with a tapping size hole using the assemble parts as a guide to ensure alignment.

Note that the carrier is additionally held by the inclusion of a toolmaker's clamp, clamping the part to the supporting bar. With the Cutter Carrier and Bearing Plate dovetails completed, check the assembly as in Photo 11. In this case the sides should be parallel, at least within 0.05mm, as the Gib Strip will not compensate for any error in this part. Ideally the rod should be at least 10mm diameter so that it rests on the two sliding faces of the dovetail. Corrections with a fine file and/or a scraper may be needed on assembly.

Having shown a toolmaker's clamp in Photo 10 this would seem an appropriate time to discuss their use in machining operations. Whilst it is considered essential for the packing used with a clamp to be just higher than the part being held, such that clamping takes place at the end of the clamp this is not so when using a toolmaker's clamp. With toolmakers clamps, the two clamp faces must sit accurately on the faces of the two items being held, SK1 seeks to make the position clear. The essential requirement is that the distance between the two arms be accurately set using the screw nearest the

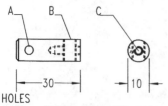

HOLES
A 4mm DIMPLE FOR GRUB SCREW
B M5
C M3 X 12 DEEP.
POSITION A AND B ON ASSEMBLY
HOLE C TO AID REMOVAL OF PART
AFTER ASSEMBLY.

MATERIAL 12mm DIAMETER
STEEL 230M07

QUANTITY 1 OFF

LEADSCREW NUT 1

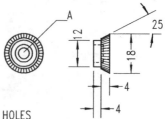

HOLES
A 5.2mm C/BORE 8.5mm 5mm DEEP

MATERIAL 20mm DIAMETER STEEL 230M07

QUANTITY 1 OFF

CALIBRATE WITH 40 DIVISIONS

DIAL 3

LEADSCREW 5

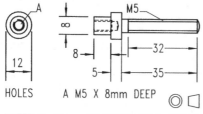

HOLES   A M5 X 8mm DEEP

MATERIAL 12mm DIAMETER STEEL 230M07

QUANTITY 1 OFF

DIAL CALIBRATION
AID SK2

clamping point. The outer screw is then used to apply the clamp force. Some reservation though should be considered when rough castings are being clamped, though in the case of Photo 5 Chapter 3 the fact that one surface was a round pillar made it a special circumstance.

The turned items

You may, as I did, use an existing arbor in which case dimensional changes are probable, otherwise make the Arbor (6) as per drawing. The essential feature is that the 25mm diameter and the taper are concentric. Holding one end in the chuck,

13. Machining the Cutter Carrier for weight reduction and better visibility when in use.

supporting the other with the tailstock centre. Turning the taper at the tailstock end and the 25mm diameter with a left hand knife tool will achieve this.

The remaining turned items need little comment. Note that the Leadscrew Nut (1) holes A and B are drilled on assembly. The 8mm length on the Leadscrew (5) should be just longer than the thickness of the Bearing Plate to permit rotation with minimal backlash. Calibration of the Dial (3) may be a problem due to the absence of a dividing head, in which case use SK2 as a temporary method as follows:- Mark the sloping face of the Dial with marking blue, centralise the Dial over the sketch and make the calibration lines using a scriber. Final calibration can be done when the Dividing Head (that follows in the next chapter) has been completed.

Final assembly

Cut a length of 10mm x 3mm steel, 75mm long and trim the ends to make the Gib Strip

(2) and assemble together with the Body and the Cutter Carrier. Fit the Gib Strip screws and tighten. Loosen screws, remove the Gib Strip, centre punch in the marks made and drill the dimples 4mm diameter to take the end of the screws. Reassemble and fully tighten the Gib Strip screws. Fit the Leadscrew Nut through the hole provided for this in the Cutter Carrier and tighten its fixing screw (H1). Loosen screw, remove Leadscrew Nut (using a long M3 screw to achieve this), centre punch where marked and drill 4mm dimple. Refit the Leadscrew Nut and fully tighten its fixing screw ensuring that it is located in the dimple just drilled.

Next task it to drill through the assembly with an M5 tapping size drill as seen in **Photo 12**. Ensuring that the machine table is clean and the Cutter Carrier is standing firmly on the table, will make certain that the hole is aligned accurately with the dovetails.

Open up the hole to 5.5mm through both the bearing plate and the Cutter Carrier and whist still assembled tap the Leadscrew Nut M5. Dismantle, make the 14mm counterbore in the Cutter Carrier and open up the hole to 8mm in the bearing plate. Assemble once more and, with the Gib Strip screws preliminarily adjusted, check that the slide works satisfactorily when turning the leadscrew.

Some scraping of the slide surfaces may be required. If everything is as it should be, lock the slide by fully tightening the Gib Strip screws and once more return to the milling machine as in **Photo 13** and machine the edges of the Cutter Carrier as per drawing. This reduces the weight of the unit and improves visibility of the cutter and workpiece.

I was pleasantly surprised how accurately

14. Skimming the sides to level up the two parts and improve appearance.

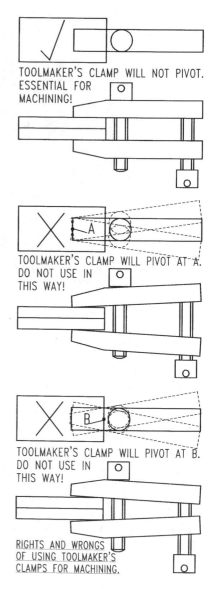

TOOLMAKER'S CLAMP WILL NOT PIVOT. ESSENTIAL FOR MACHINING!

TOOLMAKER'S CLAMP WILL PIVOT AT A. DO NOT USE IN THIS WAY!

TOOLMAKER'S CLAMP WILL PIVOT AT B. DO NOT USE IN THIS WAY!

RIGHTS AND WRONGS OF USING TOOLMAKER'S CLAMPS FOR MACHINING.

SK1

15. The finished boring head but still with temporarily calibrated feed dial.

the sides of the Cutter Carrier and body lined up, see Photo 13, but still decided to machine the side faces for appearance purposes. This is shown being carried out in **Photo 14** whether you do this yourself the option is yours. If you do, parallels are required under the assembly. Finally, dismantle, deburr sharp edges, making this a generous chamfer on the prominent edges when assembled. Clean all parts,

especially sliding surfaces, reassemble with a touch of oil where appropriate and the boring head is finished, **Photo 15**, except that is for the temporarily, calibrated dial which can be seen in the photograph.

In the next chapter the project to be started is a dividing head, this immediately making use of the boring head just completed and being used for the dial just mentioned.

1. Direct dividing with a single gear.

Chapter 7

Dividing Head

We now come to the second of the major items described in this book that still uses largely basic milling operations but provides a chance to use the boring head made in the previous chapter.

The design

This is a simple dividing head based on using a single gear, **Photo 1**, and more complex dividing using a gear train, **Photo 2**. The dividing head may find a multitude of uses, such as cutting gears, drilling holes on a pitch circle diameter, milling squares and hexagons and marking divisions on a machine slide dial. The single gear could be replaced with a dividing plate and the plunger assembly modified to suit. This would increase the number of divisions possible.

Manufacture
The Body (1)

Cut a length of 50mm square steel 108mm long, (plus an allowance for machining),

and machine the ends to a dimension of 108mm, using the set-up of an angle plate and a cylindrical square. Mark out the position for all holes, and width of 20mm grove, drill and tap holes C, a tapping size hole for D and a large pilot hole where the Spindle is to fit.

Position the part using an engineer's square, **Photo 3** and, after adding additional support to the machine table, mill the 20mm slot to the depth of 8mm using the marks to position it, **Photo 4**. It will of course be necessary to make a number of passes to mill the slot to the required depth. If you do not have a 20mm end mill or slot drill you will have to make the slot in two stages. In this case do not use a slot drill when widening the slot as this is best done using an end mill. Reposition on the table and with a large size drill open up the pilot hole, **Photo 5**. The Body is raised on parallels to avoid the drill hitting the table as it breaks through.

Now is the time to bring the boring head

HARDWARE
H1 M6 NUTS 2 OFF
H2 M6 X 20 SOCKET CSK SCREW 1 OFF
H3 M5 X 12 SOCKET CAP SCREW 4 OFF
H4 M4 X 6 SOCKET GRUB SCREW 4 OFF
H5 SPRING TO SUIT
H6 M6 X 25 HEX HEAD SCREW AND NUT 1 OFF
H7 M6 X 16 HEX HEAD SCREW AND WASHER 1 OFF

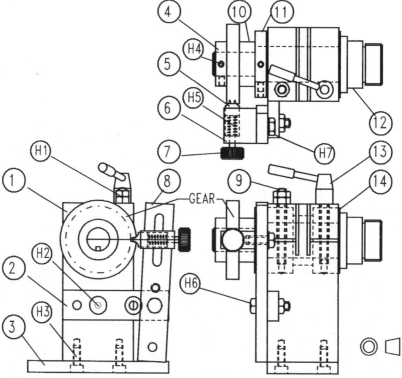

NOTE. THE DETAIL PART DIMENSIONS SUIT GEARS WHICH ARE
5/8" WIDE, SPACER WASHERS MAY BE REQUIRED WHERE
NARROWER GEARS ARE BEING USED.

DIVIDING HEAD, SINGLE GEAR DIVIDING

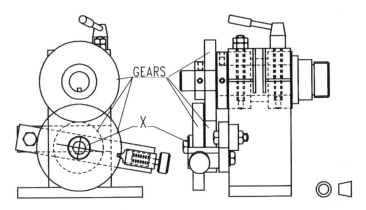

GEARS

X

NOTE. NO DETAILS ARE GIVEN FOR THE METHOD OF COUPLING THE TWO GEARS TOGETHER (X) AS IT IS EXPECTED THAT THE METHOD, AND PROBABLY THE PARTS, USED WITH THE AVAILABLE LATHE CHANGE WHEELS WILL BE USED.

DIVIDING HEAD, MULTIPLE GEAR DIVIDING

2. Fitted with gear train for more complex divisions.Below Right: 3. Positioning the Body on the machine table

63

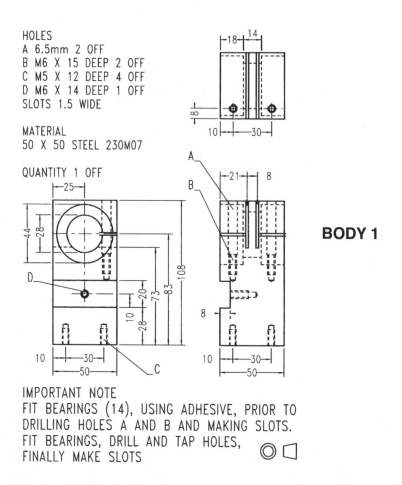

HOLES
A 6.5mm 2 OFF
B M6 X 15 DEEP 2 OFF
C M5 X 12 DEEP 4 OFF
D M6 X 14 DEEP 1 OFF
SLOTS 1.5 WIDE

MATERIAL
50 X 50 STEEL 230M07

QUANTITY 1 OFF

BODY 1

IMPORTANT NOTE
FIT BEARINGS (14), USING ADHESIVE, PRIOR TO
DRILLING HOLES A AND B AND MAKING SLOTS.
FIT BEARINGS, DRILL AND TAP HOLES,
FINALLY MAKE SLOTS

into use. **Photo 6** shows a typical set of boring tools that can be obtained, quite economically in sets, from many of the suppliers to the home workshop. With a suitable holder they can also be used on the lathe.

Fix the part to the table, **Photo 7**, taking note that the clamps used to hold the part will need to be as compact as possible to avoid fouling the boring head. Also place

three, support pieces against the Body, one on each side and one at the end as can just be seen in the photograph. Whilst supporting the part during machining they have another more important function as will be seen later.

Starting from the hole size already drilled gradually increase this to 28mm and to a depth of 35mm. It is essential that the depth stop be set, as the boring tool will

64

4. Machining a slot in the Body. Being an open ended slot an end mill can be used. Below: 5. Using a large drill to prepare the Body for boring. Right: 6. Typical set of boring head tools.

easily be bent if the tool is fed too deep into a blind hole. Boring will be a slow job as I would suggest initially that each cut be limited to around 0.2mm maximum; that would be 50 cuts to get from 24mm to 44mm. You may as your confidence grows feel able to increase this to 0.3mm, maybe more. Use the fine down feed to feed the tool. The speed should be set on the low side, say 250 rpm, but as in all cases there is justification for some trial runs at higher speeds, especially if you have obtained free cutting, 230M07 steel.

After having made a few cuts, measure the distance between the inside of the bore and the outside of the Body, the two sides

and top should be equal. As 28mm is a very generous clearance on the Spindle great accuracy is unnecessary so a rule measurement will suffice. If there is an error, reposition the table left to right and/or back to front to minimise the error. To avoid the cut becoming too intermittent, make a small adjustment only; bore to the larger size, make a further adjustment to the table position and bore again, repeat as necessary.

When the hole reaches 28mm set the depth stop to 18mm and bore to 44mm diameter. This bore should be central to a higher degree so when the hole gets to about 40mm again measure the two sides using a vernier. If the pocket will run to it, the micrometer shown in **Photo 8** is admirable for this as its round anvil permits measurements from concave surfaces. The thin anvil enables measurements from narrow slots and

7. The boring head gets its first task to perform. Below: 8. A useful micrometer for measuring from concave surfaces, also from slots and step measurement.

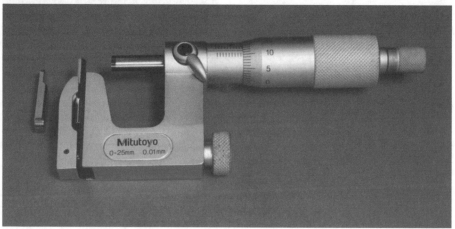

BEARING 14

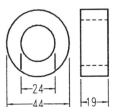

MATERIAL   ◎ ◁
50mm DIAMETER CAST IRON
BORE TO 24MM AFTER FITTING TO BODY.
INITIALLY BORE 20MM DIAMETER

QUANTITY   2 OFF

step measurements with the anvil and the clamp removed.

When the 44mm bore is finished, loosen the clamps and turn over the Body and secure and make the second bore. The purpose of the three, support pieces now becomes obvious as they will avoid the need for centring the bore once more. The two bores will be reasonably concentric although as will be seen this is not crucial.

Bearings (14)

Cast iron has been chosen for the Bearings as the dissimilar metals, cast iron and mild steel, will enable the Spindle to rotate easily, even when the Bearings are adjusted to be on the tight side. Making the Bearings is straightforward and needs no explanation, other than to say, make the outside diameter around 0.05mm smaller than the bore in the Body to allow space for a film of adhesive. Make the inside diameter around 22mm for final boring to 24mm after fitting to the Body. Fit the Bearings to the Body using a two-part resin adhesive and leave to set.

Again we set up the angle plate end on as seen in **Photo 9**. The engineer's square is being used on the base of the Body to ensure that the Spindle will be parallel to the Dividing Head base. Both Bearings are bored at this stage so the

9. Setting up the Body, now with Bearing inserts fitted.

67

cutter will need a projection of at least 52mm. Do pay attention to ensure that the revolving head does not foul with any of the assembly, studs, clamps, angle plate, etc. Bore completely through in stages to 24mm, **Photo 10**. Accurately measure the finished diameter of the bore, possibly making a plug gauge to confirm the figure. Make a note of this for use when turning the Spindle. Next drill and tap holes A and B. A milling machine accessory, not yet mentioned, is a Slitting Saw Arbor, whilst not in the essential category, it is an item that will be difficult to do without. If you do not have one then it is time to break of from this project to another, not an uncommon situation in the home workshop; this time to make such an arbor. For this task at least a 100mm diameter saw is preferable and I would suggest 1.5mm thick.

Mount the Body onto the table but

10. Final boring the Bearing inserts. Below : 11. Slitting the Body to provide the individual adjustment of each Bearing. DANGER, KEEP WELL CLEAR.

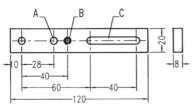

HOLE SIZES
A 6.2mm 2 OFF
B THREAD TO SUIT GEAR COUPLING USED
C 6mm WIDE SLOT

MATERIAL 20 X 8 STEEL 080A15

QUANTITY 1 OFF

DETENT ARM 8

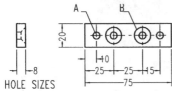

HOLE SIZES
A 6.2mm 2 OFF
B 6.2mm CSK 14mm DIAMETER 2 OFF

MATERIAL 20 X 8 STEEL 080A15

QUANTITY 1 OFF

DETENT ARM SUPPORT 2

MATERIAL
6mm DIAMETER STEEL 230M07

QUANTITY 1 OFF

STUD 9

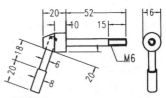

MATERIAL
16mm DIAMETER STEEL 230M07
8mm DIAMETER STEEL 230M07

DRILL AND FIT ARM ON ASSEMBLY

QUANTITY 1 OFF

LOCKING HANDLE 13

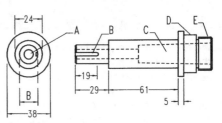

HOLE SIZES
A 8mm
B DIAMETER AND SLOT TO SUIT GEARS USED

C, D AND E AS PER LATHE SPINDLE NOSE

MATERIAL 38mm STEEL 230M07

QUANTITY 1 OFF

SPINDLE 12

some form of packing will be required due to the projection of the Bearings. Lower the saw, whilst stationary, till it just touches the top of the Body, move the saw from the Body and lower by a further 21mm plus half the thickness of the cutter. If as suggested the saw is 1.5mm, this makes 21.75mm. Make the first cut. Having made the first cut, lower the saw a further 8mm and make the second, **Photo 11**. The additional support shown on the right is probably unnecessary but I cannot stress to strongly to err on the side of caution when mounting items for milling. Actually, the ease with which a slitting saw cuts through a piece of steel is perhaps surprising and illustrates the danger present when such an item is used. Do bear this very much in mind and keep well clear whilst it is running. **Photo 12** shows the set-up for making the horizontal slots. A small piece of hack saw blade might be required to complete the slot. Clamping the part to the angle plate is best done with a bar drilled to match the pitch of the slots, do make a couple of these and keep available for future use.

Spindle (12)

I am not going into detail regarding turning the Spindle as I am assuming that you already have a good understanding of operating the centre lathe. If hesitant, then the WPS 34 in the Workshop Practice series would be helpful reading. Essentially, turn the 24mm diameter and Spindle nose whilst supported with the tailstock centre, then fit and adjust the fixed steady whilst still supported by the tailstock. Remove tailstock and bore the internal taper, **Photo 13**. Do take note that it will be necessary to set the top slide to the required angle before starting this sequence.

Mount a piece of steel on the machine table using an engineer's square to ensure the right face is in line with the cross feed.

13. Machining the Morse taper. Below Right: 14. A set up for holding round components on the machine table, typically as in Photo 15.

Add a second piece of steel to the right of the first ensuring the inner edges are parallel. To do this place a parallel between them as they are being positioned and clamped. Include a clamp in the assembly as shown in **Photo 14**. The Spindle can now be placed between the two pieces of material and clamped in position, **Photo 15**. Remember this assembly, as it is an excellent method of holding round parts on the machine table. Machine the keyway taking note that with such a small cutter, the machine speed should be set at its maximum, hopefully 2000 rpm plus.

Detent (5)

Turn the 4mm diameter and make the M4 thread. Reduce the 12mm outer diameter to 10mm and part off. Using the four-jaw chuck, and gripping the 4mm diameter, set the 10mm diameter to run true and turn the end as shown at S1, drilling hole also. This sequence ensures concentricity.

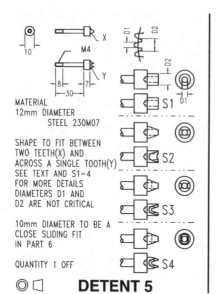

MATERIAL
12mm DIAMETER
STEEL 230M07

SHAPE TO FIT BETWEEN
TWO TEETH(X) AND
ACROSS A SINGLE TOOTH(Y)
SEE TEXT AND S1-4
FOR MORE DETAILS
DIAMETERS D1 AND
D2 ARE NOT CRITICAL

10mm DIAMETER TO BE A
CLOSE SLIDING FIT
IN PART 6

QUANTITY 1 OFF

DETENT 5

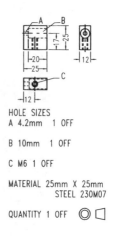

HOLE SIZES
A 4.2mm 1 OFF

B 10mm 1 OFF

C M6 1 OFF

MATERIAL 25mm X 25mm
              STEEL 230M07

QUANTITY 1 OFF

DETENT CARRIER 6

Shape the detent end using a file. Fit a washer on diameter D2 to prevent the file damaging the larger diameter. Shape as S2 until it just breaks into the hole D1. File a triangular groove so that the larger end is just larger than the hole D1 as S3. Finally,

file the outer edges such that they clear the teeth on either side when the detent locates on the central tooth, S4.

Detent Carrier (6)

Cut a piece of 25mm square 14mm long and face the two sides to give 12mm, either

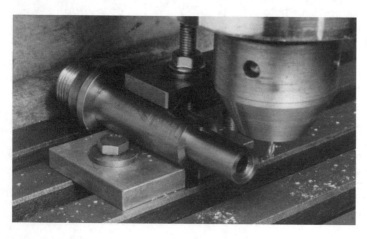

15. Milling the keyway in the Spindle.

72

MATERIAL 16mm DIAMETER
STEEL 230M07

QUANTITY 1 OFF

DETENT KNOB 7

on the milling machine or mounted in the four jaw chuck. Mark out holes A and C. Drill hole A fully through the part. Mount in the four-jaw chuck using hole A and the tailstock centre to position the part and bore 10mm hole as a close, sliding fit on the Detent. Drill and tap hole C, deburr edges.

Turned Items

The remaining turned items are simple and need no comment, except to recommend that you drill and fit the arm in the Locking Handle after assembly when the best position for this can be chosen.

Detent Arm Support (2)

Cut a length of 20mm x 8mm, 75mm long plus an allowance for machining. Machine ends, mark out, drill and countersink.

Detent Arm (8)

Cut a length of 20mm x 8mm, 120mm long plus an allowance for machining. Machine ends, mark out holes A and B and drill and tap. Mount on machine table as shown in **Photo 16** and using a slot drill make the 6mm wide slot. The cutting edge on the cutter I used became blunt on the very first cut, and got progressively worse, hence the poor finish in the slot that is evident. This resulted despite it being a brand new cutter. The lesson to be learnt is to buy the very best cutting tools you can afford thinking twice about buying economy versions.

Base (3)

Cut a length of 50mm x 8mm, length to suit the mounting conditions you wish to adopt. Machine ends, mark out holes and drill as required.

Assembly

Clean all parts, deburr where required and generously chamfer corners that are prominent in the assembled state. With the Spindle in situ fully screw in the stud and lock it home. Add the two nuts; adjust and lock them together such that the Spindle

16. Milling a slot using a slot drill. It was the first task for an economy cutter that did not last the task, hence the poor result, buy the best!

73

HOLE SIZES   A M4   2 OFF

MATERIAL 45mm DIAMETER
STEEL 230M07

QUANTITY 1 OFF

THRUST BUSH 11

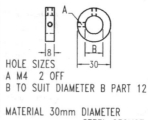

HOLE SIZES
A M4   2 OFF
B TO SUIT DIAMETER B PART 12

MATERIAL 30mm DIAMETER
STEEL 230M07

QUANTITY 1 OFF

GEAR SPACING RING 10

HOLE B
TO SUIT DIAMETER B PART 12

MATERIAL 30mm DIAMETER
STEEL 230M07

QUANTITY 1 OFF

GEAR RETAINING RING 4

becomes a little stiff to turn. Screw in the Locking Handle and tighten, mark the position where the Arm is to be, probably as in **Photos 1** and **2**, remove and drill, see **Photo 17**. Fix the Arm using a two-part adhesive.

No method of coupling the pair of gears shown in **Photo 2** has been detailed, it being assumed that, using the lathe change wheel gears, the parts from the lathe will be used. **Photo 18** shows a typical set of parts.

Finally check the engagement of the Detent with the gear wheel. If having located the Detent in one position the gear moves, when the Detent is rotated 180 degrees and re-engaged, file a very little off one side as the error indicates. Carry out this test both with the Detent between two gears and the fork across a single tooth.

In the following chapters we discuss an adaptable Grinding Rest together with some accessories to maximise the potential of the item. In this the Dividing Head is used to calibrate some micrometer dials and at the same time. final calibration of the dial on the boring head.

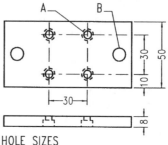

HOLE SIZES
A 5.2mm 4 OFF
   C/BORE 9mm 5.5mm DEEP

B SIZE AND POSITION, AND PART LENGTH, TO SUIT MOUNTING REQUIREMENTS

MATERIAL 50mm X 8mm
         STEEL 080A15

QUANTITY 1 OFF

BASE 3

Above: 18. A typical set of parts for linking two gears, required when setting up the dividing head as in Photo 2. Left: 17. Drilling the locking handle for its arm.

1. The complete grinding rest

Chapter 8

Grinding Rest

This final item is comprised of two sections: 1, A grinding Rest (this chapter), and 2, Accessories for the rest that enable items of tooling to be sharpened, typically end mills, lathe tools, but also simpler items such as screwdrivers.

Of all items of machinery bought, the bench grinder almost certainly falls short of that required in the home workshop by more than any other. The rest supplied is always too small and frequently insufficiently robust making it totally inadequate for serious use.

The significant feature of the rest seen in **Photo 1** is that it gives fine adjustment both to and from the front face and to and from the side face of the grinding wheel. This makes it possible to remove very small amounts whilst at the same being able to grind close up to a point, such as an adjacent cutting edge, without any fear of damaging it. To make use of this feature

the item being ground has to be held in an appropriate accessory rather than ground totally free hand.

Manufacture
The 32/50mm Square items
To economise on effort, first cut the material for parts 4, 8, 9 (2 off), 17 and 18, machining the cut faces of these as in **Photo 2**. This set up of angle plate and cylindrical square, is one with that by now you should be very much at home. However, machine one side only of items 9. Use 32mm square material for Item 8 to benefit from free cutting material, 230M07.
Slide Swivel Pieces (9)
Drill hole A and use this to mount both pieces as in **Photo 3**, use an engineer's square from the front edge of the table to ensure they are accurately placed for a later operation. Machine both edges, 16mm thick and about 14mm wide. So as not to

HARDWARE
H1 M4 X 14 SOCKET CSK SCREW 2 OFF
H2 M5 NYLOCK NUT, OR TWO LOCK NUTS
H3 M4 X 14 SOCKET GRUB SCREW AND NUT 3 OFF
H4 M4 X 6 SOCKET GRUB SCREW 1 OFF
H5 M5 X 8 SOCKET GRUB SCREW 1 OFF
H6 M4 X 14 SOCKET GRUB SCREW AND NUT 3 OFF
H7 M4 X 6 SOCKET GRUB SCREW 1 OFF
H8 M5 NYLOCK NUT,OR TWO LOCK NUTS

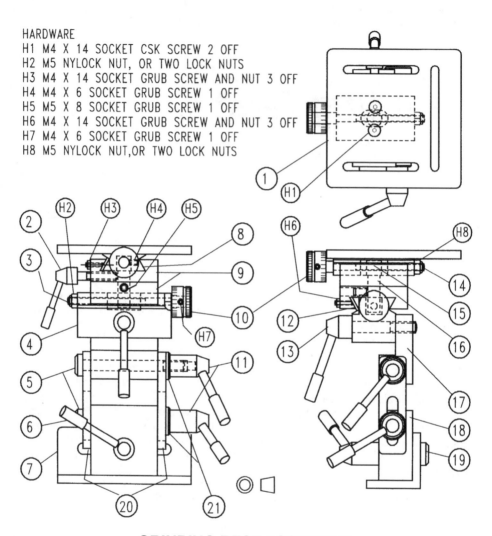

GRINDING REST ASSEMBLY

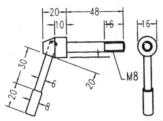

MATERIAL 8 AND 16mm DIAMETER
STEEL 230M07

QUANTITY 1 OFF

LOCKING HANDLE 13

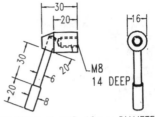

M8
14 DEEP

MATERIAL 8 AND 16mm DIAMETER
STEEL 230M07

QUANTITY 3 OFF

LOCKING HANDLE 6 & 11

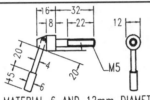

MATERIAL 6 AND 12mm DIAMETER
STEEL 230M07

QUANTITY 1 OFF

LOCKING HANDLE 2

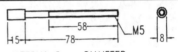

MATERIAL 8mm DIAMETER
STEEL 230M07

QUANTITY 1 OFF

LOWER LEAD SCREW 3

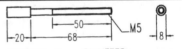

MATERIAL 8mm DIAMETER
STEEL 230M07

QUANTITY 1 OFF

UPPER LEAD SCREW 14

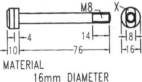

MATERIAL
    16mm DIAMETER
    STEEL 230M07

QUANTITY 2 OFF

ROUND END (FILE) AS AT X
TO FIT END OF SLOT

LOCK SCREW 5

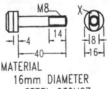

MATERIAL
    16mm DIAMETER
    STEEL 230M07

QUANTITY 1 OFF

LOCK SCREW 19

ROUND END(FILE) AS AT
X TO FIT END OF SLOT

2. Machining the ends of parts cut from 50mm Sq. bar.

lose position, clamp to the machine table as in **Photo 4** before removing the screws, and also add end supports. Using a large slot drill, mill a slot down the centre to a depth of 7.9mm. An end mill is also acceptable as the slot is open ended, although I prefer to use a slot drill. However, do not use a slot drill to widen an already formed slot, so change to an end mill and widen to give the dimensions of 10mm and 26.5mm.

I am assuming that by now your confidence in using your milling machine is sufficient for you to justify the purchase of a dovetail cutter. If not, you will have to follow the method used for the boring head. Lower the dovetail cutter into the slot by about 4mm and start machining the

3. Machining the edges of the Slide swivel pieces.

80

4. Preliminary work on the dovetails.

dovetail, doing this in stages until a flat of about 0.5mm remains along the top. Repeat this on the second side. Next lower the cutter and skim the base of the slot to establish the 8mm dimension. Using the same process as for the top half of the dovetail, machine the lower half until it becomes level with the half already produced. Now, moving the cross slide by only 0.1mm for each pass, continue until the flat is machined away. Leaving the cutter set at this height repeat the process on the first side, **Photo 5**. Mark out and drill and tap the remaining holes.

Lower Slide (4)

Position the part on the table using a dial test indicator to ensure that it runs parallel with the table traverse and securely clamp

5. Finishing the dovetails in the Slide swivel pieces.

6. Positioning the Lower slide prior to cutting the dovetails.

in place, **Photo 6**. Do equip yourself with some form of mounting a dial test indicator, such as seen in the photo, as it is so much more convenient than mounting it in the drill or cutter chuck. Set the height of the dovetail cutter using a stack of distance pieces, 20 + 3 + 0.5 giving 23.5 as seen in **Photo 7**. Produce the dovetail as in **Photo 8**. Ideally though, do this in two stages as was done for the slide swivel pieces using

the distance pieces for the second stage, and not one stage as **Photo 7** and **8** indicate. Do this by first doing stage one on both sides followed by setting the full depth as in **Photo 7** and then finishing the dovetail on both sides. This will ensure they are both at the same level.

Fit a 12mm slot drill and machine the slot, **Photo 9**, do not forget to set the table stops, (seen in the lower picture), when machining closed end slots. Having positioned one end, distance pieces to the value of 14mm will enable the other stop to be easily set. Mark out and drill holes A and B but making B tapping size for M5 at this stage.

Top Slide (8)

To reduce to 12mm after sawing to 12mm plus, clamp to the machine table with clamps on one side only and reduce half the width to 12mm. Before removing clamps fit further clamps on the already machined half and then remove first clamps. Reduce

7. Setting the depth of dovetail using distance pieces.

82

8. Cutting the dovetails in the Lower slide.

thickness of second side; do not alter down feed between machining the two halves. Machining this is now almost the equal of machining the lower slide so will not go into detail. The slot goes completely through the part so make sure you align the part with the "T" slot or use packing to raise it from the table. Again, hole A should initially be tapping size for M5.

Upper Arm Spacer (17)

Set this up as shown in **Photo 10**, only a single clamp has been used as there is insufficient space to take a second. Because of this do use a substantial clamp and position the part close to the clamping stud as shown. The support pieces are also absolutely essential. Mill the step as shown ensuring that you cut towards the support. Then mount onto an angle plate and machine the two angled faces. Mark out and drill and tap holes A and B.

Lower Arm Spacer (18)

After machining as indicated on Page 77,

it only remains to mark out and drill holes.

Side Arms (20)

Position a clamp on the angle plate using an engineer's square as shown in **Photo 11** using this to support the arms whilst machining their ends. Remember to machine towards the support as shown in **Photo 12**. However, the photographs show that I had second thoughts having moved

9. Cutting the slot in the lower slide.

83

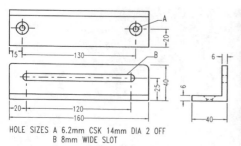

HOLE SIZES A 6.2mm CSK 14mm DIA 2 OFF
        B 8mm WIDE SLOT

MATERIAL 40 X 40 X 6 BRIGHT ANGLE

QUANTITY 1 OFF

BASE ANGLE 7

10. Machining the Lower arm spacer. With only one clamp being used the supports are essential for added security whilst machining.

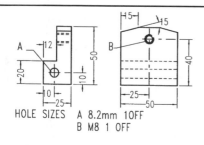

HOLE SIZES A 8.2mm 1OFF
          B M8 1 OFF

MATERIAL 50mm SQUARE STEEL 230M07

QUANTITY 1 OFF

UPPER ARM SPACER 17

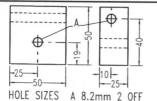

HOLE SIZES A 8.2mm 2 OFF

MATERIAL
50mm SQUARE STEEL 230M07

QUANTITY 1 OFF

LOWER ARM SPACER 18

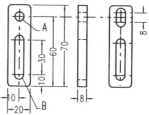

ARM Y   ARM Z

HOLE SIZES A 8.2mm 1 OFF
          B SLOTS 8mm WIDE

MATERIAL
20mm X 8mm STEEL 080A15

QUANTITY 1 OFF ARM Y
          1 OFF ARM Z

SIDE ARMS 20

84

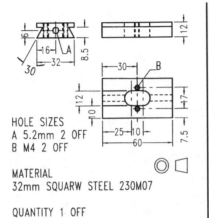

HOLE SIZES
A 5.2mm 2 OFF
B M4 2 OFF

MATERIAL
32mm SQUARW STEEL 230M07

QUANTITY 1 OFF

TOP SLIDE 8

HOLE SIZES
A M4 1 OFF

CALIBRATE WITH 40 DIVISIONS

MATERIAL 25mm DIAMETER
STEEL 230M07

QUANTITY 2 OFF

FEED KNOB 10

MATERIAL
20mm DIAMETER STEEL 230M07

QUANTITY 2 OFF

LOCK SCREW WASHER 21

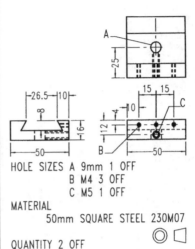

HOLE SIZES A 9mm 1 OFF
         B M4 3 OFF
         C M5 1 OFF

MATERIAL
    50mm SQUARE STEEL 230M07

QUANTITY 2 OFF

SLIDE SWIVEL PIECES 9

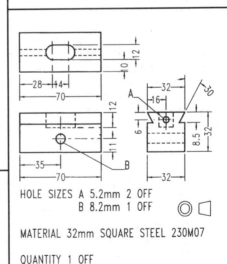

HOLE SIZES A 5.2mm 2 OFF
         B 8.2mm 1 OFF

MATERIAL 32mm SQUARE STEEL 230M07

QUANTITY 1 OFF

LOWER SLIDE 4

Above: 11. Setting up a support for machining the Side arms. Above Right: 12. Machining the ends of the Side arms. Some second thoughts obviously resulted in the set up being changed between Photos 11 and 12.

the angle plate and the clamp is fitted higher. This does though remind me to comment that much mounting work on the angle plate can be carried out remote from the machine. This can be on the surface plate, or even mounted in the bench vice with the working face horizontal, making positioning parts very much easier in many cases.

Milling Vice - required or not?

You may have become aware that we have already carried out a wide range of milling activities, yet still without using a vice. I have deliberately done this to highlight the fact that a vice is far from essential, it would though not be appropriate to overlook its use.

Numerically, the disadvantages of using a vice far outnumber the advantages, but it depends on how much emphasis you place on each factor. The major advantage of the milling vice is speed of use, but only where positioning the vice is not critical and positioning the part in it is straightforward. Its disadvantages are cost, time consuming to position it accurately on the table and difficulty in many cases of positioning the part in the vice, especially for batch production. For many, the disadvantages will be outweighed by the advantages even if its use will be limited to a small fraction of the work undertaken. At first, for limited use, it may appear that a vice from the cheaper end of the market will suffice, these will normally be offered as drilling machine vices. Without doubt the most likely limiting factor regarding these is jaw lift, as illustrated in **SK1**. In the case of the milling vice this problem is largely eliminated by fitting a much longer moving jaw. **SK2**.

Next requirement for a milling vice is accuracy, with two factors being particularly important. These are, that the vertical jaw face must be truly at right angles with its

base and that the face on which the jaw slides must be parallel to the base of the vice. The reason for this requirement is that this face is often one on which the workpiece rests, either directly or with parallels interposed.

The next requirement is that it should be sufficiently robust. Most milling vices

13. Modified drilling vices make adequate vices for vertical milling.

owe their design to their intended use on the horizontal mill where loads will often be much greater than loads present in vertical milling. A milling vice is therefore frequently more robust than required. My approach was to modify a pair of the cheap and

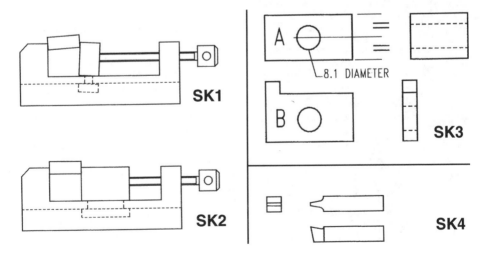

SK1

SK2

A

8.1 DIAMETER

B

SK3

SK4

cheerful drilling vices by skimming all relevant surfaces to improve accuracy and by adding a much longer moving jaw, **Photo 13**. These vices, available for less than a £10, look fragile but their large footprint, low slung design and four widely spaced fixings make them more than adequate for the task, if modified as suggested. When re-machining them the front edge of the base was also machined parallel with the fixed jaw face. This makes positioning them on the machine table an easy task, **Photo 14**.

Photo 15 shows the smaller vice being used to hold one of the side arms for slotting, though the task could have been done more easily with the part mounted on the machine table. The parallels would have been slid out before the cutter broke fully through.

Table (1)

Cut a piece of 100mm x 6mm, 100mm long plus an allowance for machining and place this on the machine table as shown in **Photo 16**. Line up the edge to be machined with the gap of a "T" slot so that the cutter will not damage the table and machine the edge, **Photo 17**. Back in Chapter 2 regarding "T" nuts I indicated that an improved finish can result if a light finishing cut, say 0.1mm, is taken where the traverse direction and cutter rotation are the same. This is a chance to try this out for yourself, do remember that you need a sharp cutter for this process.

Mark out, drill and countersink the two holes and once more accurately position the part on the machine table. This time packed up to allow for milling the through slots, **Photo 18**. Set the table traverse stops, and cross feed stops if your machine has them, (typically as seen at bottom of

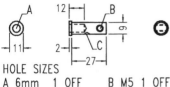

HOLE SIZES
A 6mm 1 OFF   B M5 1 OFF

C 5mm DIAMETER DIMPLE 1 OFF

POSITION B AND C ON ASSEMBLY

MATERIAL 12mm DIAMETER
STEEL 230M07

QUANTITY 1 OFF

LOWER LEADSCREW NUT 16

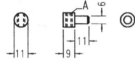

HOLE SIZES
A M5 POSITION ON ASSEMBLY

MATERIAL 12mm DIAMETER
STEEL 230M07

QUANTITY 1 OFF

UPPER LEADSCREW NUT 15

Above Left: 14 Having its front edge parallel with the vice jaws enables the vice to be positioned with ease. Left: 15 Milling the slots in the Side arms (though this operation could easily have been done with the part. mounted on the machine table). Note the cross feed stops at the bottom of the photograph set up to control the length of the slot.

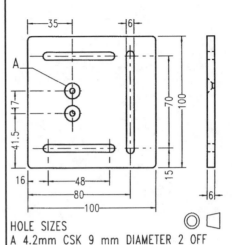

HOLE SIZES
A 4.2mm CSK 9 mm DIAMETER 2 OFF

MATERIAL 100mm X 6mm STEEL 080A15

QUANTITY 1 OFF

TABLE 1

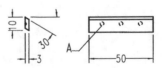

HOLE SIZES
A DRILL DIMPLES AFTER
ASSEMBLY TO TAKE END
OF ADJUSTING SCREWS

MATERIAL 10mm X 3mm
STEEL 080A15

QUANTITY 2 OFF

GIB STRIP 12

Photo 15) enabling the slots to be cut without continual reference to the table traverse dials. At 6mm diameter you will need a speed on the high side, say 1000rpm plus.

Base Angle (7)
By this stage of the series, machining the base angle should come as second nature. **Photo 19** shows the set up for machining the slot.

16. Positioning the Table in preparation for machining its edges.

Lock Screws (5 and 19)
The turned parts are all quite simple and therefore I do not intend to go into the lathework involved in these. However, the Lock Screws do have a little milling activity that could present a problem to the novice. The lesson here is that what may seem to be a problem when attempting to use the available methods for holding a part (angle plate, vice, etc.) can become a very straightforward operation if aided by a simple home-made fixture.

Make the two items shown in **SK3** taking note that the hole must be central in item A, all other dimensions can suit available material, a length of tube will also be required. Set these up on the mill table and with a 4mm mini mill running at maximum speed mill the flat as shown in **Photo 20**. Now turn over the lock screw complete with holder A and relocate against the stop in part B making the operation of milling the second side, and

17. Machining the Table's edges.

18. Milling the Table slots.

Below Right: 19. Milling the slot in the Base angle.

the remaining two screws, a very simple operation.

Gib Strips (12)

These may appear to present a problem if a tilting vice is not part of your kit, you have though already made the ideal fixture for holding these. Clamp one of the Slide Swivel pieces to the machine table and with a round rod and a piece of packing use this to hold the Gib Strips for machining, **Photo 21**. Turn strips over and machine the second side. What appeared a problem has turned out to be very simple. When on your own, do not lose sight of the fact that a part already made can often assist in machining other parts that follow.

Feed Knob (10)

Calibrating the Feed Knob can be the first task for your recently made Dividing Head. After boring and making the knurl whilst mounted in the chuck, mount on a taper stub mandrel and turn the portion to be calibrated. Do ensure that the knob is very firmly pushed onto the mandrel. Without removing from the chuck, transfer chuck, mandrel and knob to the Dividing Head and

mount this on the lathe as shown in **Photo 22**.

This is your first opportunity to check the accuracy of the Dividing Head mandrel. Set up a dial test indicator on the surface to be calibrated and rotate the Dividing Head by hand noting any deviation present. If the dial runs perfectly true you have indeed done well but some small error is likely which in most most cases, even when making a

20. Set up for machining the Lock screw using the parts illustrated in SK3.

gear, will not be of any consequence.

It is easy to fall into the trap of thinking that a pointed cutter should be used to make the lines on the dial. However, an error in concentricity will cause the line to change in width as the dial rotates. Make a cutter as **SK3**; I would suggest a tip width of 0.2 to 0.3mm. Depending on the error in concentricity you may still need to make slight changes in the depth of cut as the dial rotates. I would suggest you find the mid-point of any error and set the depth of cut at this point to be 0.1mm. Make sure the tool is firmly clamped on the top slide and use its calibration to set the line lengths. With an M5 thread having a pitch of 0.8mm, 40 calibrations will give increments of 0.02mm.

You can now go back to the dial on the boring head and calibrate this also. You will though need to mount it on a taper stub mandrel and re-machine the sloping face, even if you had not temporarily calibrated this.

21. Using one of the Slide swivel pieces as a fixture for holding the Gib strips for machining the angle on their edges.

92

Assembly

First, assemble both items 9 together with item 16 and fit and lightly tighten the screw H5. Take apart and drill dimple C in part 16 as indicated by the mark made by the screw. Reassemble with items 4, 8, 12, and 15 added making sure that screw H5 locates in the dimple and tighten Gib Strip screws so that the slides are firmly fixed. Drill through items 4 and 8 into the Leadscrew Nuts (items 15 and 16) using an M5 tapping size drill. Open up holes in items 4 and 8 to 5.2mm diameter and tap the Leadscrew Nuts M5 through the holes just drilled. This will ensure satisfactory alignment. Dismantle and drill the dimples in the Gib Strips as indicated by the screw marks.

Assemble the parts involved in using the Locking Handles and mark the preferred position for their arms, remove, drill and fix the arms using two-part resin

22. Calibrating the Feed knob using the Dividing Head made in the previous part of the series.

adhesive. You will see from the **Photo 1** that I chose to fit the top Locking Handle 11 on the left rather than on the right as shown in the assembly drawing. This helps to make them both more accessible. It is important to take note that items must return to the same position as variations in the position of their threads will also cause handle arm positions to vary. I would suggest marking them with one, two and three centre punch marks in some obscure position, such as on the threaded ends of the lock screws. Assemble for the last time applying a little oil in appropriate positions and the Grinding Rest is complete, only now waiting the arrival of its attachments for sharpening various metalworking and woodworking tools. These will be described in the following chapters.

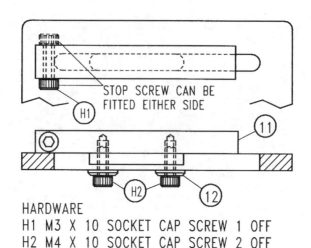

STOP SCREW CAN BE
FITTED EITHER SIDE

HARDWARE
H1 M3 X 10 SOCKET CAP SCREW 1 OFF
H2 M4 X 10 SOCKET CAP SCREW 2 OFF

FENCE AND STOP ASSEMBLY AS1

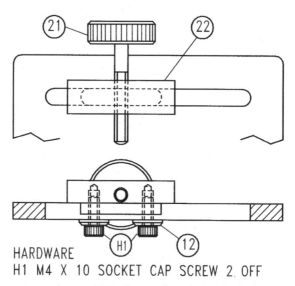

HARDWARE
H1 M4 X 10 SOCKET CAP SCREW 2 OFF

CLAMP SCREW ASSEMBLY AS2

Chapter 9

The Grinding Rest
Minor Accessories

In the last chapter we completed the adjustable off-hand grinder rest, the full extent of its capability will though only be achieved by the addition of various accessories, these being the subject of this and the following chapter.

At this stage, description of the manufacturing processes will be kept to a minimum, as by now these should not present a problem. Making them will though continue to provide valuable necessary experience. Much of the chapter will centre on the use of the accessories and includes photographs to illustrate the operations that can be performed. First however, very important safety considerations must be aired.

IMPORTANT SAFETY REQUIREMENTS
• *Do wear safety spectacles or facemask.*

• *Due to the item being ground often being unsupported close to the wheel when using the accessories, only take very light cuts. The depth of cut must be controlled by the fine feed and the fence rather than manually.*

• *Make multiple passes where more material has to be removed than can be taken safely at a single pass.*

• *Keep the overhang of the tool, from the accessory holding it to a minimum.*

• *In view of the overhang do ensure the accessory is held firmly down on the rest's table.*

• *Keep the table and the sliding surfaces of the accessory as free of grinding dust as possible. This will result in easier hand feeding and makes for safer working.*

• *When the grinder is running do not make adjustments to the rest, other than using the table's fine feeds.*

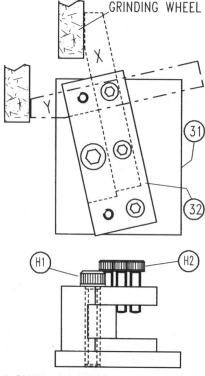

GRINDING WHEEL

X

Y

31

32

H1   H2

X. POSITION FOR SHARPENING SIDE AND TOP
CLEARANCES AND RELIEF.
Y. POSITION FOR SHARPENING FRONT
CLEARANCE AND RELIEF.

THE FIXTURE IS GUIDED BY A FENCE MOUNTED
ON THE REST TABLE USING THE SWIVEL BASE
(21) TO SET THE ANGLE. THIS IS ALSO USED
WITH OTHER FIXTURES BUT FOR SIMPLICITY IS
NOT INCLUDED ON THEIR ASSEMBLY DRAWINGS.

HARDWARE
H1 M6 X 30 SOCKET CAP SCREW 1 OFF
H2 M4 X 16 SOCKET CAP SCREW 3 OFF

SQUARE WORKPIECE
HOLDER ASSEMBLY AS3

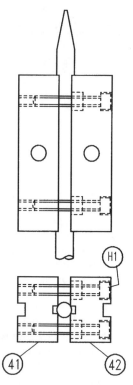

H1

41   42

HARDWARE
H1 M4 X 25 SOCKET
CAP SCREW 4 OFF

ROUND WORKPIECE
HOLDER ASSEMBLY AS4

96

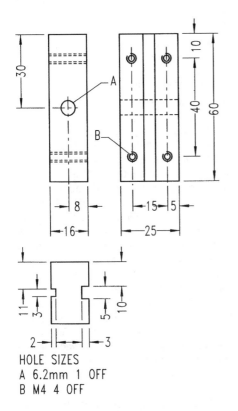

HOLE SIZES
A 6.2mm 1 OFF
B M4 4 OFF

MATERIAL
        25mm X 16mm STEEL 080A15

QUANTITY 1 OFF

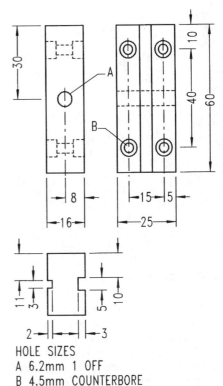

HOLE SIZES
A 6.2mm 1 OFF
B 4.5mm COUNTERBORE
        7.5mm X 5mm DEEP BOTH SIDES

MATERIAL
        25mm X 16mm STEEL 080A15

QUANTITY 1 OFF

SIDE ONE 41   SIDE TWO 42

1. Milling the web on the fence.

Make sure that all locking levers are firmly tightened before starting the grinder. The rest can be used as a conventional off-hand Grinding Rest in which case ensure that the front edge of the table is no more than 1mm from the grinding wheel and the item being ground supported by the rest's table.

Due to grinding dust getting into the locking lever assemblies they can become difficult to undo, but becoming free quite suddenly as more force is applied. This can cause rapped knuckles with unpleasant results. Make a lever extension as per SK1 to prevent this. Do not though use it for tightening the levers as this may result in over tightening.

As the Grinding Rest is not directly mounted off the bench grinder it is essential

that both be mounted on a very robust base. If this is not done the rest will be able to move relative to the off-hand grinder when in use. At best this may result in inaccurate results but much worse, be the cause of a serious accident.

The accessories
Fence and stop assembly, AS1
This is an essential part of the system being used to accurately guide the part being ground, either across the face of the wheel or down its side. A stop screw can be fitted when required to ensure that the part being ground cannot pass beyond a certain point.

Throughout the book, I have emphasised that much milling work can be carried out without using a vice as the work holding device, perhaps to the point of giving the idea that it is not an essential requirement. Where a vice comes into its own is with the smaller items, which are more difficult to hold by other means. The Adjustable Fence (11) is a typical instance. Machine lower web **Photo 1**. Turn over, hold on web just made, and machine top surface to reduce thickness to 6mm. Drill and tap holes. Radius web ends using a file.

The assembly also requires some turned washers. However, where simple parts are required throughout the rest of the book, I will not comment on them in the text, the drawings should give all the information required.

Photo 2 shows the fence fitted, this can of course be in any one of the three slots. The web, which fits into the slot, is shorter than the slot permitting coarse adjustment of the stop screw position; final adjustment will be achieved using the fine feed facility of the rest. You may find it easier to fit the

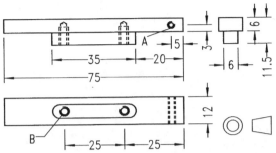

HOLE SIZES A. M3 1 OFF B M4 X 8 DEEP 2 OFF

MATERIAL 12mm SQUARE STEEL 230M07

QUANTITY 2 OFF

ADJUSTABLE FENCE 11

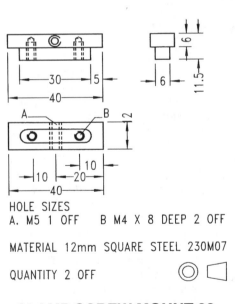

HOLE SIZES
A. M5 1 OFF   B M4 X 8 DEEP 2 OFF

MATERIAL 12mm SQUARE STEEL 230M07

QUANTITY 2 OFF

CLAMP SCREW MOUNT 22

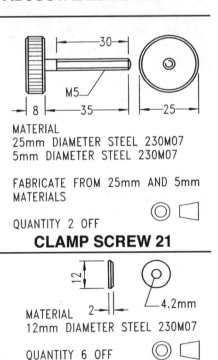

MATERIAL
25mm DIAMETER STEEL 230M07
5mm DIAMETER STEEL 230M07

FABRICATE FROM 25mm AND 5mm
MATERIALS

QUANTITY 2 OFF

CLAMP SCREW 21

MATERIAL
12mm DIAMETER STEEL 230M07

QUANTITY 6 OFF

WASHER 12

2. Fence fitted to the rest's table. Note the stop screw at the left hand end.

fence (and clamp screw assembly AS2) to the table if you remove the table (2 screws) from the remainder of the rest. When fitting the fence in either of the side slots, it should always be fitted such that if the base moves away from the fence, the item being sharpened moves away from the wheel, not towards it.

Swivel Base Clamp Screw, AS2

This enables an accessory to be fixed to the rest's table where the accessory itself feeds the workpiece; typically when using the end mill sharpening assembly as will be seen in the next chapter.

Manufacture of the Clamp Screw Mount (22) follows very closely that for item 11 above.

Square Workpiece Holder and Swivel Base, AS3

The main purpose of the holder is to mount square section lathe tools but no doubt other uses will surface. The Base (31) is used for setting the angle of the workpiece relative to the feed direction and is also used with many of the remaining accessories. For simplicity it is not shown on their drawings but can be seen in the photographs.

To machine the square Workpiece Holder (32) mount on an angle plate using a parallel to ensure the part is parallel to the machine table. Commence machining groove with an 8 or 10mm slot drill, working to the 5mm dimension. Open up to 13mm using an end mill. Drill and tap holes. Cut a length of 50 x 6mm for the Swivel Base (31) Machine ends to 75mm, again using the angle plate for mounting. Drill and tap holes.

To sharpen a lathe tool, mount the holder on the swivel base at an angle to suit the tool's side relief with the rest's table angled left to right to suit the tool's side

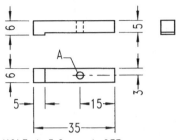

HOLE A 3.2mm 1 OFF

MATERIAL 6mm SQ. STEEL 230M07

QUANTITY 1 OFF

LEAF SPRING CLAMP 53

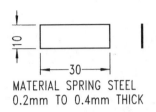

MATERIAL SPRING STEEL
0.2mm TO 0.4mm THICK

QUANTITY 1 OFF

LEAF SPRING 52

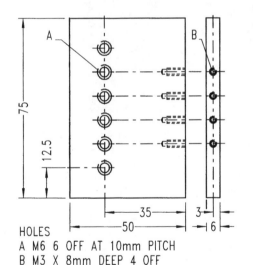

HOLES
A M6 6 OFF AT 10mm PITCH
B M3 X 8mm DEEP 4 OFF

MATERIAL 50mm X 6mm STEEL 080A15

QUANTITY 1 OFF

SWIVEL BASE 31

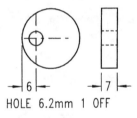

HOLE 6.2mm 1 OFF

DIAMETER TO SUIT
SLITTING SAW BORE

MATERIAL STEEL 230M07

QUANTITY 1 OFF FOR
EACH BORE SIZE

PIVOT 51

clearance. **Photo 3** shows this operation.

If you have studied the Grinding Rest in detail you may consider that the angle set using the swivel base would actually be achieved using the rest's swivel facility. This is not so, its use, with a few exceptions, is purely to set the approach angle of the face being ground to the wheel.

When grinding a portion from the side of a workpiece it would seem obvious that the feed direction should be parallel to the side of the wheel, SK2A. However, any small error in the approach angle could cause the part to be additionally ground on its side, SK2B. In view of this, feed direction

is deliberately set to an angle to the side of the wheel to avoid this possibility SK2C. This may seem like a procedure to overcome the accuracy limitations of the home workshop, it is though standard practice in industry. D, E and F show the same situations relative to the front face of the wheel. This angle, set by the rest's swivelling facility, should be a maximum of a degree or two.

Round Workpiece Holder AS4

This is normally mounted on the swivel base, similar to using the square workpiece holder, and is used typically for holding screwdrivers, a wheel dresser and round

102

section lathe tools, etc.

Cut two lengths of 25 x 16mm, one each for Side One (41) and Side Two (42). Using an angle plate for supporting parts, machine ends and grooves. Grooves must be central otherwise they will not align if one part is turned over relative to the other. Drill, tap and counterbore.

When using it to sharpen a screw driver (**Photo 4**) the holder will need to be removed from the swivel base, turned over, and the second side ground. This will necessitate the fine left to right feed being adjusted again as it is unlikely that the result on both sides will be the same without this being done.

The screw driver end will now require grinding to bring the thickness to that required. Remove the holder from the swivel base turn on its side and grind the end to establish the required blade width. Due to the overhang of the screwdriver from

4 Sharpening a screw driver.

5 A parallel end to the screw driver is easily achieved, not the case when attempting this by unassisted off hand grinding

6. The accessory used for the screw driver is also used to hold the wheel dresser.

the holder, DO NOT be tempted to feed this free hand; even for this simple operation it is safer to use the fine feed, assisted by the fence, making multiple passes until the required blade width is achieved.

Sharpening a screw driver free hand may seem like a simple exercise but anyone who has tried it will have experienced the difficulty of getting the two sides parallel. **Photo 5** illustrates how a good result can be achieved, and simply, with this accessory. The photograph also shows a centre punch, which will be discussed later.

Other typical uses are wheel dressing, **Photo 6**, (note this still uses the fence and the swivel base) and sharpening round lathe/boring tools. Note that, with the fence mounted at right angles to that in the photo and the wheel dresser turning through 90 degrees on the swivel base, the right hand side of the wheel can be dressed. However, dressing the side should be kept to an

absolute minimum, as it will reduce the width of the wheel and therefore its strength.

Slitting Saw Sharpening assembly AS5
This comprises the swivel base with a few simple parts (51, 52 and 53) added.

The method for sharpening slitting saws should be clear from **Photo 7**. Do remember that the saw is fed by hand with the swivel base held firmly against the fence and the saw against the swivel base. The inward fine feed is used to control depth of cut. With the large teeth on the saw no stop is required. However, with an accurately dressed wheel, saws with very small teeth can be ground when a stop, fitted to the fence, will be necessary to avoid the wheel touching the adjacent tooth. In this case the left to right feed would be used to accurately set the stop position. The bush on which the saw rotates is drilled off centre to provide adjustment for differing saw diameters. The leaf spring may require

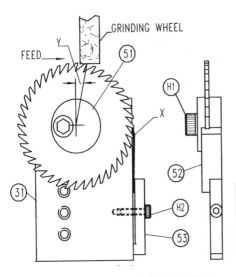

SLITTING SAW SHARPENING ASSEMBLY AS5

bending at "X" as shown, to improve indexing on smaller tooth saws.

This completes the minor assemblies all of which can be seen in **Photo 8**.

End mills and Slot drills

Whilst many items, typically lathe tools, screw drivers, etc., can be sharpened free hand with some success, this is almost impossible in the case of end mills and slot drills. An accessory enabling these to be sharpened, both on their end teeth and cutting edges, is the subject for the next chapter.

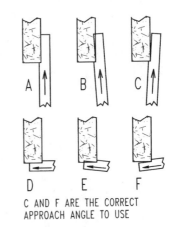

C AND F ARE THE CORRECT
APPROACH ANGLE TO USE

WORKPIECE APPROACH ANGLE SK2

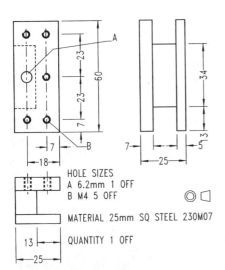

HOLE SIZES
A 6.2mm 1 OFF
B M4 5 OFF

MATERIAL 25mm SQ STEEL 230M07

QUANTITY 1 OFF

SQUARE WORKPIECE HOLDER 32

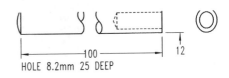

HOLE 8.2mm 25 DEEP

LOCKING LEVER EXTENSION SK1

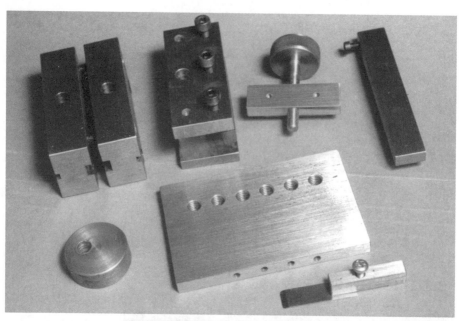

Above: 8 The minor accessories. Right: 7 Sharpening a slitting saw.

Chapter 10

The End Mill Sharpening Fixture

We now come to an End Mill Sharpening fixture, AS6 by far the most complex of the accessories. This enables both the end and side cutting edges to be sharpened but can also be used where a round workpiece needs to be rotated, typically a centre punch.

The accessories thus far are quite simple as can was seen in Photo 8 Chapter 9; they will though dramatically improve results compared to totally free hand grinding. The item shown in **AS6** is though quite different with some comparatively complex parts to be made. It will though make it possible to sharpen end mills, a task that is impossible free hand.

Spindle (62)
Cut a length of 30mm diameter, 105mm long. Mount in the three-jaw chuck supporting the outer end with a steady. Face, drill and tap M8 15mm deep. Remove and firmly fit a short hexagon head screw in the tapped hole, and grip this in the three-jaw again supporting the outer end with a

steady. Face then centre drill the end, remove steady and support with the tailstock centre. Turn the 100mm length to 24mm diameter, leaving the flange at the tailstock end. Check before reaching the 24mm diameter that the result is parallel. This is essential so that the spindle slides in its bearings without stiffness or shake. A small error can be eliminated by careful use of very fine emery cloth.

Whilst still supported by the tailstock centre, fit and set the fixed steady at the tailstock end. Remove the centre, set top slide to 5 degrees, machine the bore and leave the top slide at this angle for making the collets. Drill 8mm to a depth that just contacts the end of the screw. Remove from chuck and screw from spindle and return spindle to chuck, now holding it on the 24mm diameter, (suitably protected), drill through 8.2mm.

Collets (80)
As these are used when sharpening the cutting edges of an end mill, concentricity is essential, as it is also with the 24mm

1. Turning the collets from a longer piece of material supported by the fixed steady minimises material wastage.

diameter and the taper bore of the Spindle. To achieve this, outer diameters and bore must be made without removing the part from the lathe. Using a fixed steady and a long length of material, **Photo 1**, will avoid leaving a short stub in the chuck as each collet is parted off. Machine outer diameters and bore. **Photo 2** shows a bull nose tool being used to form the collet's waist. Do make all the collets you are likely to require

at this stage whilst the top slide is set at the 5 degree angle.

Slotting the collets is another task needing to use the Dividing Head made earlier. Make a collet holding jig as **SK1** using an M5 screw to fix the collet to this, mount in the three-jaw and slot as **Photo 3**.
Bearings (65)
Take a piece of 40mm diameter cast iron, 38mm long, and mount in the lathe chuck,

2. Turning a collet's waist.

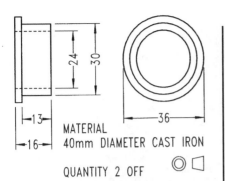

MATERIAL
40mm DIAMETER CAST IRON

QUANTITY 2 OFF

BEARINGS 65

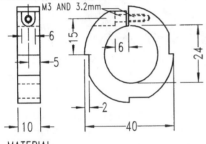

MATERIAL
40mm DIAMETER STEEL 230M07

QUANTITY 1 OFF

ADDITIONAL COLLERS MAY BE REQUIRED
FOR USE WITH CUTTERS HAVING MORE
THAN FOUR CUTTING EDGES.

4-WAY INDEXING COLLAR 61

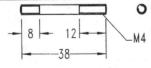

MATERIAL 4mm DIAMETER
STEEL 230M07

QUANTITY 1 OFF

FRONT BEARING STUD 66

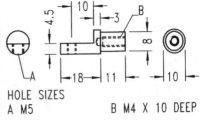

HOLE SIZES
A M5   B M4 X 10 DEEP

MATERIAL 10mm DIAMETER
STEEL 230M07

QUANTITY 1 OFF

INDEX ARM SUPPORT 68

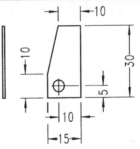

HOLE SIZE 5.2mm

MATERIAL 0.5 SHEET STEEL

QUANTITY 1 OFF

INDEX ARM 67

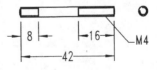

MATERIAL 4mm DIAMETER
STEEL 230M07

QUANTITY 1 OFF

REAR BEARING STUD 76

3. Slotting a collet using the dividing head made earlier in chapter 7.

Below Left: 4. Boring the bearing supports.

if a smaller three-jaw is all that is available, you will probably have to use the reverse jaws. Using a larger four-jaw with the jaws in the more normal position will be an advantage. Drill through, say 12 to 16 mm, and bore 24mm diameter 18mm deep, use the spindle as a gauge. Face end, turn 30mm diameter by 13mm long. Remove from the chuck, reverse, refit, make second bearing repeating the above sequence, additionally reduce the outer diameter to 36mm diameter.

The advantage of using the four-jaw now becomes obvious, if you are using this with the jaws placed normally it should be acceptable to part the two bearings on the lathe. However if you are using the reverse jaws in the three-jaw, I would be hesitant to recommend this due to their limited length of grip. In this case remove from the lathe and saw in half, return and face sawn ends to give the 16mm length.

Front/Rear Bearing Supports (63/64)

Cut two pieces of steel, surface the cut edges, drill and tap smaller holes. Mark out position for the 30mm hole, drill 6mm

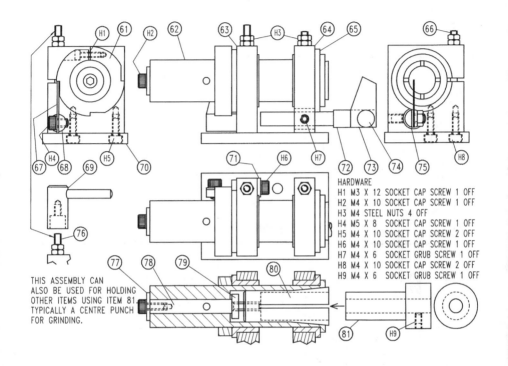

THIS ASSEMBLY CAN ALSO BE USED FOR HOLDING OTHER ITEMS USING ITEM 81. TYPICALLY A CENTRE PUNCH FOR GRINDING.

HARDWARE
H1 M3 X 12 SOCKET CAP SCREW 1 OFF
H2 M4 X 10 SOCKET CAP SCREW 1 OFF
H3 M4 STEEL NUTS 4 OFF
H4 M5 X 8 SOCKET CAP SCREW 1 OFF
H5 M4 X 10 SOCKET CAP SCREW 2 OFF
H6 M4 X 10 SOCKET CAP SCREW 1 OFF
H7 M4 X 6 SOCKET GRUB SCREW 1 OFF
H8 M4 X 10 SOCKET CAP SCREW 2 OFF
H9 M4 X 6 SOCKET GRUB SCREW 1 OFF

END MILL SHARPENING ASSEMBLY AS6

diameter. Place a short length of 6mm rod through the two holes to align them and mount on the faceplate.

Carefully advance the tailstock centre into the 6mm hole to centralise it and firmly clamp parts in place. Push a length of bar through the lathe mandrel bore from the changewheel end, to make the short length of rod available for removal. Balance faceplate assembly.

Open up the 6mm hole with the largest drill available. Mount the boring tool, and

111

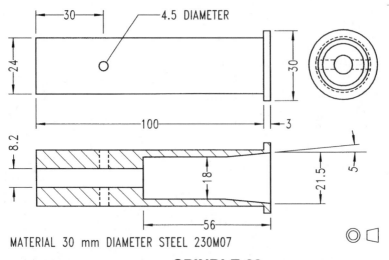

MATERIAL 30 mm DIAMETER STEEL 230M07

QUANTITY 1 OFF **SPINDLE 62**

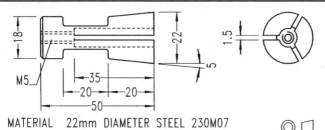

MATERIAL   22mm DIAMETER STEEL 230M07

MAKE ONE TO SUIT EACH CUTTER TO BE HELD MAKING THE
WAIST DIAMETER TO CREATE A WALL THICKNESS OF 1mm.

COLLET 80

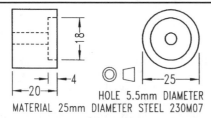

HOLE 5.5mm DIAMETER
MATERIAL 25mm DIAMETER STEEL 230M07

COLLET HOLDING JIG SK1

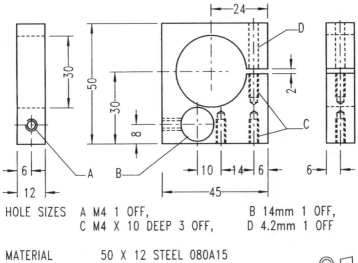

HOLE SIZES   A M4 1 OFF,   B 14mm 1 OFF,
                 C M4 X 10 DEEP 3 OFF,   D 4.2mm 1 OFF

MATERIAL   50 X 12 STEEL 080A15

QUANTITY 1 OFF

FRONT BEARING SUPPORT 64

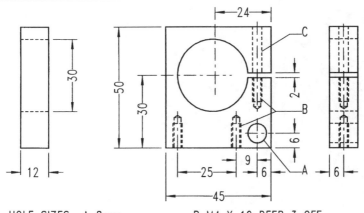

HOLE SIZES   A 8mm,   B M4 X 10 DEEP 3 OFF,
                 D 4.2mm 1 OFF

MATERIAL   50 X 12 STEEL 080A15

QUANTITY 1 OFF   **REAR BEARING SUPPORT 63**

5. Setting up the bearing supports for machining their base.

with the lathe stationary bring the tip of the tool up to the faceplate surface at some available point. Adjust the saddle stop, also using the top slide to make the final adjustment. Make a gap of 0.05mm to ensure the tool will not foul with the faceplate. If you are not happy working this close to your faceplate when blind, you could add a thin piece of card between the part and the faceplate to give more leeway. Bore to a diameter about 0.05mm larger than the bearing outer diameter, **Photo 4**. If you do not have a 14mm drill you will also need to bore the 14mm hole in part 64. Fit bearings using two part resin adhesive.

To ensure the spindle rotates and slides freely without shake it is essential that both bearings be at the same height, the following ensures this.

Mount the two bearings on an angle plate using the spindle to align the bearings.

6. Machining both bearing supports at one time ensures that both bearings will be precisely at the same height.

114

Do this with the angle plate mounted in the vice as in **Photo 5** this is much easier than performing the task with the angle plate surface vertical. This process may seem a simple, risk free task though there is one point that must be observed. The fixings in the base of the two parts must be aligned correctly when mounting the parts on the angle plate, or the bearings will not be in line when mounted to the base (70). Note that the right hand hole B in part (63) is 15mm from the edge whilst the left-hand hole in part (64) is 20mm. This means that the pitch between them must be accurately set to the difference of 5mm. With this done, the bearings should easily align, with a little help from the clearance in the fixing holes. Machine the base of the bearing supports, **Photo 6**.

Indexing Collars (61)
Turn one or more collars as required. Make a stub mandrel for mounting the collar on the three-jaw chuck and mount on the dividing head for milling the ratchet teeth. **Photo 7** shows a simple method of

Above Right: 7. A simple, but reasonably accurate, way of positioning a cutter relative to a round workpiece, in this case an indexing collar.

8. Machining the teeth on an indexing collar.

9. Machining the screw head recess in an indexing collar.

positioning the cutter in preparation for milling the ratchet's teeth. Clip the rule onto the square at the required dimension and place the square against the part being machined and the cutter against the end of the rule and you are ready for machining, simple! **Photo 8** shows the teeth being cut.

Whilst still mounted on the dividing head, machine the recess for the screw head, **Photo 9**. Marking out for drilling the tapped hole can be a little tricky but making a 6mm diameter bush, and using this as a drill bush, makes the process simple, **Photo 10**. Drill, tap and slot collar.

Remaining parts

The remaining parts are all relatively simple and experience gained thus far should enable them to be easily completed. One point though worthy of mention relates to machining the flat on the Index Arm Support (68). Machining the flat is of course a simple

exercise but how is such a small item securely held. As mentioned in a previous chapter do not lose sight of the fact that quite often another part being made may be able to hold a part that would otherwise be difficult. **Photo 11** shows how the rear bearing support (63) makes the task of

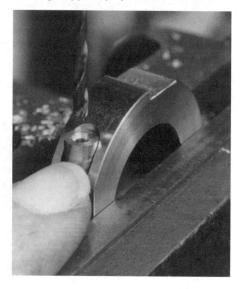

*10. A small bush avoids the need to mark
'out (not an easy operation) the position
for the clamping screw.*

116

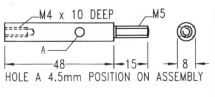

M4 x 10 DEEP   M5

A

48   15   8

HOLE A 4.5mm POSITION ON ASSEMBLY

MATERIAL 8mm DIAMETER STEEL 230M07

QUANTITIY 1 OFF

COLLET DRAW BAR 78

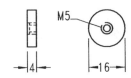

M5

4   16

MATERIAL
16mm DIAMETER STEEL 230M07

QUANTITY 1 OFF

COLLET EXTRACTOR BUSH 79

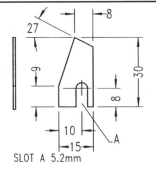

8

27

9   30

8

10

15   A

SLOT A 5.2mm

MATERIAL 0.5mm SHEET STEEL

QUANTITY 1 OFF

TOOTH REST 73

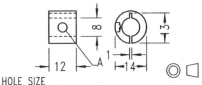

8   3

12   A   1   14

HOLE SIZE
A 4mm 2mm DEEP, POSITION ON ASSEMBLY

MATERIAL 16mm DIAMETER STEEL 230M07

QUANTITY 1 OFF

TOOTH REST SUPPORT CLAMP RING 75

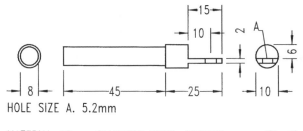

15

10   2   A

45   25   10   6

8   10

HOLE SIZE A. 5.2mm

MATERIAL 10mm DIAMETER STEEL 230M07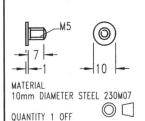

QUANTITY 1 OFF

TOOTH REST SUPPORT 72

M5

7   10

1

MATERIAL
10mm DIAMETER STEEL 230M07

QUANTITY 1 OFF

TOOTH REST SCREW 74

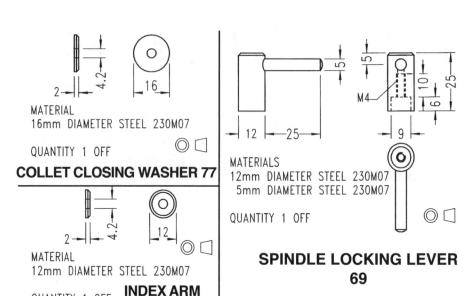

MATERIAL
16mm DIAMETER STEEL 230M07

QUANTITY 1 OFF

COLLET CLOSING WASHER 77

MATERIALS
12mm DIAMETER STEEL 230M07
 5mm DIAMETER STEEL 230M07

QUANTITY 1 OFF

MATERIAL
12mm DIAMETER STEEL 230M07

QUANTITY 1 OFF

INDEX ARM SUPPORT WASHER 71

SPINDLE LOCKING LEVER 69

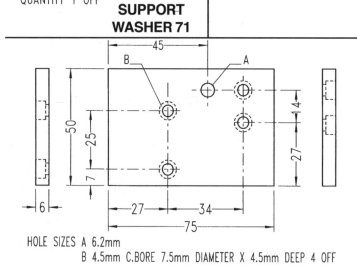

HOLE SIZES A 6.2mm
          B 4.5mm C.BORE 7.5mm DIAMETER X 4.5mm DEEP 4 OFF

MATERIAL 75mm X 6mm STEEL 080A15

QUANTITY 1 OFF

BASE 70

118

holding item 68 easy.

The Tooth Rest Support (72) whilst similar, is longer, and can better be held using the method illustrated by Photo's 14 and 15, Chapter 7.

The hole in item (78) is drilled on assembly using the spindle (62) as a guide. The purpose of this is, with a small bar through the two items, to enable the screw H2 to be tightened on assembly.

Having completed the assembly, **Photo 12**, there only remains a need for an explanation as to how this is used to sharpen end mills and slot drills. This, together with a few other operations, will be covered in the next chapter.

11. The rear bearing support makes an excellent fixture for holding the index arm support while machining the flat.

12. The finished accessory together collets for various cutter shank sizes and a 6 way indexing collar.

119

Chapter 11

Using the End Mill Sharpening Fixture

This chapter provides instruction for using the End Mill Sharpening Fixture detailed in the last chapter.

Setting the angles

A necessary requirement for using the grinding rest, is to be able to reasonably accurately set the angle between the rest's table and the face and side of the grinding wheel. Using the protractor from a combination set or some other engineer's protractor may seem like the device to use to measure the angle but their bulky nature will make them very inconvenient in practice. To overcome this, make some gauges, as per **SK1** and as seen in **Photo 1**.

To set the angle relative to the side of the wheel, bring the table close to the face of the wheel and check the angle as per **SK2**. Setting the angle relative to the face of the wheel is more complex as the angle is continually varying round the curvature of the wheel. Grinding on the face will though only be used where a very narrow land is being ground, typically, the end teeth of an end mill. As a result, only the angle at the point where grinding takes place is of importance. Provisionally set up the accessory with the device being ground and measure the distance above the table that grinding will take place. Mark the required gauge at this height and use it to set the table's angle such that gauge and wheel touch at this point, as shown in **SK3**.

Sharpening End Mills and Slot drills

End teeth

Fit the end mill accessory with the four tooth indexing collar ensuring that there is no end float and adjust the bearings so that the spindle rotates freely but without shake. Fit the end mill making sure that the end teeth are horizontal and vertical when the

1. These simple angle gauges are essential for setting up the grinding rest.

index collar is located against the index arm and lock the spindle.

Set the end mill accessory on the swivel base to an angle of approximately 2 degrees to ensure that the end teeth will be slightly concave when ground.

Fit the fence to the table with the stop screw at the left-hand end. Set the table at 90 degrees to the side of the wheel and 5 to 6 degrees relative to its face at the point where grinding will take place, see **SK3**. With the swivel base against the fence and the stop, and the end mill very close to the face of the wheel, adjust the left right traverse such that, when grinding, the wheel will not touch the adjacent end tooth, **Photo 2**. Err on the side of caution, fine adjustment is carried out once grinding takes place. At this stage the adjustments are made with the grinder at rest. Do not forget to set on the angle of a degree or two using the rest's swivel facility and make sure that all adjustments are firmly locked.

Now with the grinder running and the swivel base held firmly against the fence and stop, very slowly advance the end mill

using the fine feed until the first sparks appear. Move the end mill to the right and place on a very small cut, about half of one division. Now slowly feed the end mill to the left until the stop is reached, ensuring that the swivel base is being held firmly against the fence and the tabletop during the operation. Remove assembly from the

2. Sharpening an end mills end teeth.

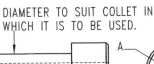

DIAMETER TO SUIT COLLET IN
WHICH IT IS TO BE USED.

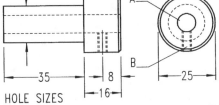

A

B

|←—35—→|←8→| |←—25—→|
|←16→|

HOLE SIZES
A TO SUIT DIAMETER OF ITEM TO BE HELD
B M4 1 OFF

MATERIAL 25mm DIAMETER STEEL 230M07

QUANTITY 1 OFF EACH DIAMETER REQUIRED

ROUND WORKPIECE
HOLDER 81

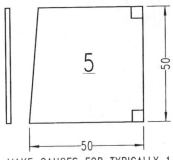

5

|←——————50——————→|

50

MAKE GAUGES FOR TYPICALLY 1,
2, 3, 4, 5, 6, 8, 10, 12, 15,
20 AND 25 DEGREES

MATERIAL
GOOD QUALITY CARD
OR ALUMINIUM 1 – 2mm THICK

QUANTITY
1 OFF EACH ANGLE REQUIRED

ANGLE GAUGES SK1

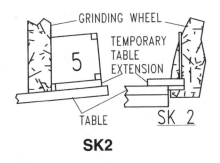

GRINDING WHEEL

TEMPORARY
TABLE
EXTENSION

5

TABLE   SK 2

SK2

GRINDING WHEEL

SK3   10

TABLE

MARK GAUGE AT HEIGHT
AT WHICH GRINDING IS
TO TAKE PLACE

table, check to see if the whole length of the end tooth has been ground and the adjacent end tooth not touched. Make adjustments to the left right traverse if necessary.

Without making further adjustments, rotate the end mill ensuring that it is locked at each position and grind the remaining three end teeth. Inspect the result and if necessary, slightly advance feed and regrind all four teeth, repeat until a satisfactory result is achieved. Adjust infeed by no more that half a division at each grinding.

3. sharpening an end mills cutting edges.

If the width of the ground surface is greater than 1.5mm then the secondary clearance should be ground. To do this repeat the above sequence but with the angle set at 10 to 12 degrees. Do this until the width of the primary clearance (that first ground) is no more than 1mm. This will ensure that the primary clearance can be ground a few times without the need to grind the secondary clearance.

In most cases sharpening the end teeth only will produce a marked improvement in the cutter's performance and will be all that is necessary. However, where the cutting edges are well worn, sharpening these will be beneficial. This will change the outer diameter and will probably be undesirable in the case of a slot drill. The outer diameter of an end mill is rarely crucial and can be sharpened on

its cutting edges without causing a problem.

Cutter edges

Swing the index arm away from the index collar, which should also be loosened and moved towards the end of the spindle. Fix the collar at a position that will enable the spindle to move lengthwise, by an amount approximately 5mm greater than the length of the end mill's cutting edges. The spindle must slide through the bearings easily but without any shake. An essential requirement for this to be achieved is for the spindle to be thoroughly cleaned of all grinding dust. Do not be tempted to lubricate the assembly, as the oil will only hold onto any grinding dust, which falls on the spindle. Fit the tooth rest support to support the end mill at its outer end and adjust the height so that the end teeth are horizontal. This can all be done with the accessory away from the grinding rest.

Set the table at an angle of 85 degrees relative to the left side of the grinding wheel. Fit the fence, with stop screw, in the right hand slot and rotate the table so that the fence is at an angle of about 1 degree to the side of the grinding wheel. Fit also the clamp screw assembly.

Fit the end mill accessory as shown in **Photo 3** making sure that there is clearance between cutter and wheel. Make sure all adjustments are tightened and that the cutter's edge is against cutter rest, and then start the grinder. Using the left to right fine feed, feed the table until the first sparks appear.

When I first attempted to carry out this operation I started at the outer end of the end mill, sharpening towards the shank end, and found it almost impossible to feed

4. Using the end mill fixture for sharpening a centre punch.

the end mill satisfactorily. After many attempts I began to feel that I was onto a looser. Alterations to the end of the tooth rest (73) had little or no effect. Without reasoning why, I decided to attempt to start from the shank end and work towards the outer end, the difference was immense. What was beginning to look an impossible task had now become a task that could be carried out with ease. Why this is I am not sure, though in the first case the mill rotates with the wheel and the operator has to keep the cutter against the rest as well as feed it along the length. In the second it rotates against the wheel which keeps the cutter against the rest and the operator needs only to make the feed.

Having successfully ground the first edge rotate the spindle anti-clockwise and grind the second followed by the third and fourth edges. However any attempt to turn the spindle whilst in the position for grinding will cause the rest to be forced into the

wheel and ground away. The assembly must therefore be moved away from the wheel but do not do this using the fine feed as back lash, etc., may make it difficult to get back to the same position. This will result in cutter edges being at differing diameters. Instead, loosen the clamp screw, move cutter assembly from the wheel, rotate cutter, replace and re-tighten clamp screw. The fence is fitted with the stop screw to ensure that the assembly returns exactly to the same position for each cutting edge. After completing the four edges, inspect the result and, if considered appropriate, repeat the procedure taking another light cut to each cutting edge, no more than half a division, probably less.

If this results in a ground width of greater than 1.5mm set the angle to 10 degrees and grind the secondary clearance to reduce the land to no more than 1mm.

For me, having started the exercise with what seemed insurmountable problems, the quality of the finished task was extremely satisfying. Whilst not appearing up to the standard of a new cutter the difference was not that great. In terms of cutting ability the difference would be hard to tell.

Centre Punch

The end mill accessory can also be used when sharpening other round tooling, a centre punch being a typical case. I considered that such situations might surface over time, many being of a different diameter. The effort of making a collet for each one as the need arises would probably be a deterrent from using the set-up. Because of this I chose to use a simple adapter (Round Workpiece Holder 81), as concentricity would often not be that important.

Photo 4 largely shows all that is needed in terms of how the task is

completed. It is worth highlighting that this is one application where the angle on the item being ground can be set using the swivel facility of the grinding rest itself. This is evident from Photo 5 Chapter 9 which clearly shows that a first rate job can be achieved.

Many other uses

The tasks possible will not stop at those already described, others surfacing with time. These using new accessories for the job in hand or ones already made. One such situation is seen in **Photo 5**. The swivel base together with half of the round workpiece holder is being used to grind the secondary angle of woodworking chisel.

The approach angle of a degree or two, set by the rest's swivelling facility, will result in a concave surface, greater than on previous tasks due to the width of the chisel.

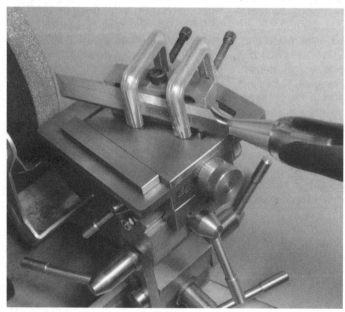

5. Sharpening a woodworking chisel.

Whilst not evident initially it will be when the cutting edge is honed on the flat stone. For quality woodwork, both primary and secondary angles should be honed the initial concave nature of the secondary angle will be removed. Keeping the approach angle as small as possible, without it being negative, will of course limit the effect.

This now completes the projects included to provide a wide and sizeable milling involvement. However, having finished with an emphasis on tool sharpening I am very briefly including in the final chapter details of how to adapt a basic off-hand bench grinder for fitting cup wheels and saucer wheels. This does not involve any milling activity but very nicely completes the equipment for tool and cutter grinding.

Whilst I have covered the mechanics of tool and cutter grinding I have included very little regarding characteristics of the cutters edges, angle, width, etc. This is a vast subject and is more than can be covered as part of this book. A good starting point is to observe the angles present on a new cutter, or even the used cutter if the wear is not excessive, and try to replicate these. Frequently articles, hobby or industrial, on the subject are far from precise with good reason. The perfect angle is so dependant on many factors, such as material being machined, but fortunately quite wide deviations from the perfect will still give very good results. There is therefore no need to be unduly concerned regarding angles; a cutter with a sharp edge but with an angle which deviates a little from the perfect will still cut infinitely better than a cutter with the perfect angle but a blunt cutting edge.

SAFETY

I make no apologies for once more bringing up the question of safe working with this grinding rest. The rest, having many more adjustments than a conventional, off-hand grinder rest and its method of use being so different, the safety considerations are also different and more importantly, greater. Do therefore read and reread the safety comments, which were included at the beginning of Chapter 9.

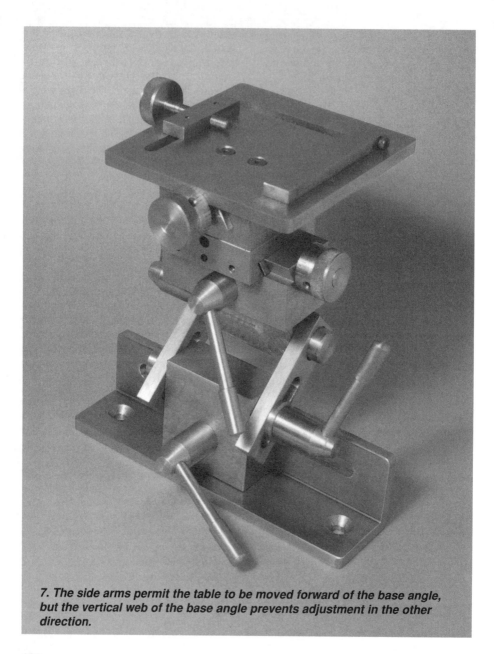

7. The side arms permit the table to be moved forward of the base angle, but the vertical web of the base angle prevents adjustment in the other direction.

Chapter 12

Tool and Cutter Grinding Head

The subject of this chapter requires no milling machine activity and because of this is not strictly appropriate to the purpose of this book. I am including it because of the connection with the content of the last three chapters.

Having put to use the grinding rest described in the previous chapters I was more than delighted with the results. However, using a standard off-hand grinder, I soon became aware that having both cup and saucer wheels available would improve its use still further. This is not surprising, as such wheels are standard practice for serious tool and cutter grinding. I therefore obtained a small (125mm) off hand grinder which I converted to take the cup and saucer wheels.

Normal practice when using these, which have larger centre holes, is to fit them with permanent adaptors. These enable wheels to be interchanged quickly and with

only minimal need of truing up. I have included dimensioned, part drawings though these will need to be checked for your own situation. The dimensions suit a 12mm spindle and a wheel hole size of 32mm.

The step in the spindle, against which the wheel flange adjoins, was not well made and more important only 1mm high so was improved by the addition of the Spindle Bush (1). I did not though consider this alone was adequate and machined the bush's face, whilst in situ, using the grinder's own motor for power. The spindle was also 1/2in diameter and I reduced this to 12mm to ensure it ran true and both ends were the same size. The following is the suggested sequence to adopt.

Grinding machine spindle

Make both Spindle Bushes (1). Cut a piece of tube to length. Set up grinder on lathe

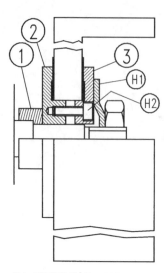

H1 EXISTING FLANGE
H2 M4 X 12 SOCKET
CAP SCREW

CUP WHEEL FLANGE ASSEMBLY

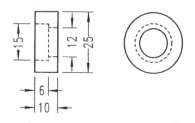

MATERIAL
25mm DIAMETER STEEL 230M07

QUANTITY 2 OFF

SPINDLE BUSH 1

1. Machining the face of the added bush powered by its own motor, the spindle was machined in a similar manner.

bed (see later comments) and machine the first end to 12mm diameter. Whilst the grinder is on the lathe, fit first bush using two part resin adhesive, holding this in place using the piece of tube and the spindle nut and leave for a few hours. Remove nut and tube and lightly machine the bush's face, **Photo 1**. Remove grinder, turn round, refit and repeat sequence on the second end making sure that both ends are the same diameter.

Mounting the Grinder

Mounting the grinder will depend both on the type of lathe bed and the form the grinder base takes, as a result precise details cannot be given. On the plus side, only very light cuts will be taken so the security of the mounting will not be severely tested. Because of this, no mater what form the bed takes, adequately mounting the grinder should not present a problem. If the bed ways are rectangular then four small toolmaker's clamps make an ideal method.

Alternatively, if the grinder has a two screw mounting, then a length of steel of suitable width could be tapped to take two fixing screws as illustrated in SK1 or, if four hole fixing, with clamp bars as in SK2. If the lathe has a Vee bed format then probably these methods could be adopted using some additional packing. If concerned about possible damage to the slide ways some thin card packing will eliminate the possibility. Having said that the mounting will not be called upon to withstand heavy loads, do not be complacent. Do give the spindle of the grinder a good tug to check adequacy of mounting prior to machining.

When mounted the spindle should run parallel to the lathe's axis. Using a surface gauge, with the two pins lowered and against the lathe's bed, check the position of the spindle at both ends as seen in **Photo 2**. When setting up for machining the second end, allowance must be made for the different spindle diameters, use feeler gauges at one end to compensate for the difference.

Inner and Outer Flanges (2 and 3)
The essential requirement for these is for their bore, the face which contacts the wheel and that which locates against the spindle bush, to be true and parallel and the 32mm diameter concentric with the bore.

Cut four pieces of 60mm diameter, place in the three-jaw and face one side of each. Then reverse, making sure that the

Above Right: 2. Setting up the grinder on the lathe bed for machining the spindle and added bush. Right: 3. A stub mandrel is used for holding the flanges for machining.

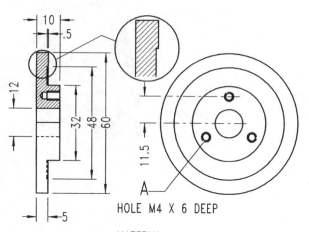

HOLE M4 X 6 DEEP

MATERIAL
60mm DIAMETER STEEL 230M07.

QUANTITY 2 OFF

INNER FLANGE 2

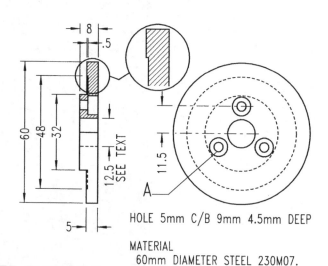

HOLE 5mm C/B 9mm 4.5mm DEEP

MATERIAL
60mm DIAMETER STEEL 230M07.

QUANTITY 2 OFF

OUTER FLANGE 3

4. The dividing head, described in chapter 7, mounted on the lathes cross slide for marking out the three holes in the flanges.

already machined face sits cleanly on the chuck jaws. Face the second side to 10 and 8mm thick, also bore each to a little under 12mm. It is essential that the hole in all four flanges finish up the same size. To achieve this, continue opening up the fourth flange to 12mm diameter and leave the boring tool set at this diameter. Replace each flange in turn and open up to 12mm at one pass. Note that the outer flange is opened up to 12.5mm at a later stage.

Make a 12mm Stub Mandrel using a piece of material at least 25mm diameter. Face and tap the end M8 then turn a 12mm stub 7.5mm long. The 12mm diameter must be a close fit in the flange's holes. Do not remove mandrel from the chuck until all flanges have been machined.

Fit the first flange and machine to the 32mm and 5mm dimensions, make also the 0.5mm deep recess, **Photo 3**. Repeat for the remaining flanges. Return the two outer Flanges (3) to the chuck and open up bore

to 12.5mm as per the drawing. Drill, tap and counter bore as required. Using a centre drill and the dividing head described in Chapter 7 mounted on the lathes cross slide, position the holes as shown in Photo 4. For this arrangement I added an additional hole in the body of the dividing head for easy fixing, see the single stud fixing visible in the photograph.

The Wheels

Whilst not readily available from most suppliers to the home workshop, the wheels required are widely used in industry and should therefore be available from your local (or maybe not so local in remote areas) abrasives supplier. The following are those that I used though your supplier may offer something different, albeit only slightly: **Taper cup wheel**, Type 11, 125mm outer diameter, 40mm outer depth with a stated hole size of 31.75mm, grade WA60 KV1. **Saucer wheel**, Type 12, 125mm outer

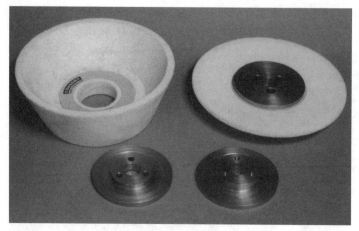

5. The two grinding wheels and the flanges for adapting the large hole in the wheels onto a smaller spindle diameter. Below: 6. The rest and grinder mounted on a purpose made base. For safety a wheel is mounted only at the end in use.

diameter, 13mm outer depth with a stated hole size of 31.75mm, grade WA60 KV1. Both stated a hole size of 31.75mm but both measured 32mm).

As an alternative to the taper cup (Type 11) a straight-sided cup could be considered, this would be a Type 6. The outlines published in this chapter show the more appropriate DIN ISO 525 shapes that are available.

If you adapt a 150mm grinder there is no need to increase the diameters, as both sizes will run at the same speed, around 2950rpm. The larger

wheels are also likely to be much more expensive, and maybe more difficult to obtain.

Mounting the wheels

Fix the flanges to the wheels ensuring that the supplied paper disks, known as blotters, are used. Very lightly tighten each screw in turn then gradually increase the tightness of each screw, again in turn. They should be tightened sufficiently to securely hold the assembly together without movement, certainly not as tight as would be done with a metal to metal assembly. Over tightening must be avoided! Then, using one of the flanges supplied with the grinder mount the assembly onto the spindle as shown in the assembly drawings. Again do not over tighten, just sufficient to ensure reliable rotation of the wheel. **Photo 5** shows the two wheels, one already fitted with its flanges.

Mounting the grinder

Both grinder and rest need to be mounted on the same rigid base. Any flexibility will cause problems with finish and accuracy, and maybe safe working. For this use Melamine faced chipboard using two boards laminated for extra rigidity. These are held together using wood screws from below at the four corners, and with the grinder's and rest's fixing screws also helping. To cope with the fixing screws and nuts that would project on the underside, the edges are finished with strips of softwood; these, being wider than the thickness of the two boards, raise the assembly off the work surface.

Direction of rotation

I have read articles, which mention the need

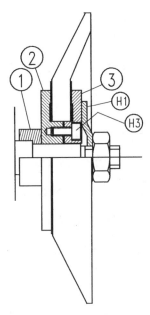

H1 EXISTING FLANGE
H3 M4 X 8 SOCKET
   CAP SCREW

SAUCER WHEEL FLANGE ASSEMBLY

for cutter grinder spindles to be reversing. This caused discussion on the advisability of this when using a single central nut for fixing the wheel as it may tend to come loose. In this arrangement there will be no problem as, in effect, we have two spindles their direction of rotation differing from end to end. As a result the spindle has left and right hand threads to cope safely with this situation.

Mounting the Rest

Mounting the rest with the grinder follows

DIN ISO 525
GRINDING WHEEL SHAPES

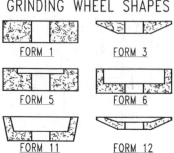

FORM 1

FORM 3

FORM 5

FORM 6

FORM 11

FORM 12

THE SHAPES ILLUSTRATED ARE JUST
A FEW OF THOSE AVAILABLE.
THEY ARE THOUGH, THOSE MOST
APPROPRIATE TO THE HOME
WORKSHOP

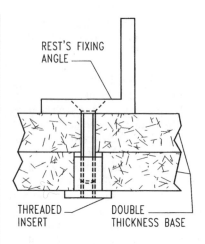

REST'S FIXING
ANGLE

THREADED
INSERT

DOUBLE
THICKNESS BASE

SK3

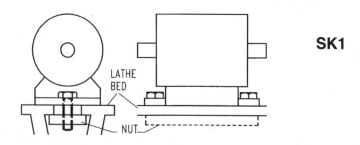

SK1

LATHE
BED

NUT

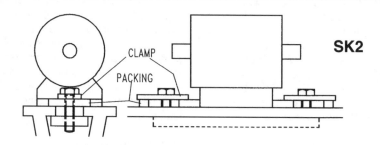

SK2

CLAMP

PACKING

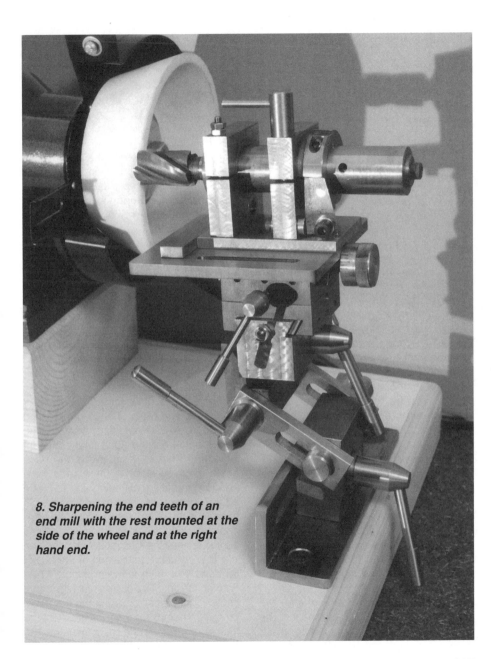

8. Sharpening the end teeth of an end mill with the rest mounted at the side of the wheel and at the right hand end.

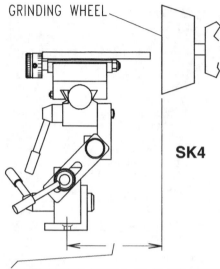

GRINDING WHEEL

SK4

THIS DIMENSION SHOULD BE IN THE ORDER OF 100MM, EITHER TO THE FLAT FACE OR CURVED FACE OF THE WHEEL DEPENDING ON THE POSITION THE REST IS MOUNTED

the same basic set-up as was illustrated in the earlier chapters. However, a second position for the rest is provided at the grinder's side, as approaching the cup wheel from this angle will be beneficial in some instances. The mountings should also be repeated at the left-hand end. **Photo 6** shows the set-up. For ease of use, push-fit inserts in the lower board as shown in SK 3 as this will avoid the need to gain access to nuts on the underside.

If you obtain a 125mm grinder it is likely that the rest may be a little on the high side and may also be for a 150mm grinder. This can be overcome by using a suitable piece of wood as a packer.

I have not given dimensions for the assembly, as they will depend on the dimensions of the grinder being used.

However, the design of the rest does only provide for it to advance the table in front of the base angle as can be seen in Photo 7, Page 128. SK4 therefore suggests a dimension relative to the wheels.

Guarding

I have, chosen to retain the guards that were part of the original grinder. These, I suspect, could be improved upon but feel that only with experience of use, will I understand the level of access to the wheels required. I would though suggest that as removal and fitting of the wheels is easy, that only the wheel being used should be fitted. This leaves the second spindle without a grinding wheel preventing the possibility of accidental contact.

Using the set up

Methods for using the rest will differ little from those described in the earlier chapters so have not included any further instructions, I have though included two photographs to show it in action. Photo 8 shows the end teeth of an end mill being sharpened whilst Photo 9 shows its cutting edges being ground. One final comment regarding Photo 8, this shows the base angle mounted close to the boards edge enabling the lower clamping arm to rotate a full 360 degrees. This makes it possible to remove the bulk of the rest from the base angle, making it easier to move the base angle between the four, mounting positions.

Having come to the end of the book I do hope you have found it useful. Whilst reading the chapters can do much to impart knowledge, actually making the items will drive this home and help considerably to increase your confidence in using the milling machine.

9. With the wheel moved to the left hand end and the rest in the front position the cutting edges are being ground.